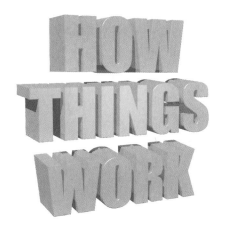

WICKED WHEELS

Steve Parker

DP

DEMPSEY
PARR

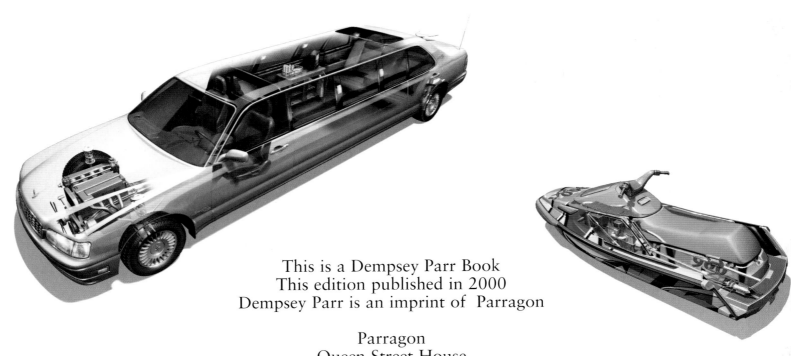

This is a Dempsey Parr Book
This edition published in 2000
Dempsey Parr is an imprint of Parragon

Parragon
Queen Street House
4 Queen Street
Bath BA1 1HE, UK

ISBN 1–84084–857-X

Printed in Dubai, U.A.E.

Produced by
Monkey Puzzle Media Ltd
Gissing's Farm
Fressingfield
Suffolk IP21 5SH
UK

Illustrations: Studio Liddell
Designer: Tim Mayer
Cover design: Victoria Webb
Editor: Linda Sonntag
Editorial assistance: Lynda Lines and Jenny Siklós
Indexer: Caroline Hamilton
Project manager: Katie Orchard

CONTENTS

GETTING AROUND

EARLY WHEELS

Our modern world runs on wheels. But wheels have not always been with us. The first wheels turned around but lay flat. Potters made bowls and vases on them in the Middle East more than 5,000 years ago. Then some whiz kid in Ancient Sumeria had the idea of turning a wheel on its edge and fixing it to a cart. With another three similar wheels at the other three corners, the cart could roll along. This was a great advance on dragging heavy loads. Soon wheels were turning on war chariots, farm wagons, and royal coaches.

POWER TO THE PEOPLE

For the next 49 centuries or so, wheeled vehicles moved by people or animal power, especially horses and oxen. In the 1800s, a human-powered vehicle was developed with two wheels and pedals, which we still use today as the bicycle. Then, just over one century ago, in the 1880s, early self-propelled road vehicles appeared. They were powered by new types of engines using liquid fuels. They were developed by German engineers Gottlieb Daimler, Karl Benz and in the 1890s, Rudolf Diesel. These strange. noisy, slow, rattling vehicles were called "horseless carriages"—a term since shortened to "car."

VEHICLES GALORE

Many other road vehicles were soon developed, such as eighteen-wheelers, trucks, coaches, and off-road vehicles, such as jeeps and tractors. Now there are at least 30 main kinds of vehicles on our roads, from bikes and motorcycles to eighteen-wheelers and flatbed semis. This book shows many of them, the parts they are made of, how they work, and what they and their drivers do.

Racing bike
With no brakes or gear changers, this bike would be very dangerous on the roads. However, its frame shape and the light-but-strong carbon fiber construction may find their way into the designs of popular mass-produced cycles.

Traffic Jam
Everyone would probably like to travel in the lap of luxury in their own personal limousine. But traffic jams would be ten times worse than they already are.

4

ON THE RIGHT TRACKS

The car was not the first engine-driven vehicle. In the early 1800s, stationary steam engines were used in mines to pump out water. Wagons with metal wheels that ran on metal tracks were also used in mines, pulled by people or ponies to haul coal and rocks. In 1804, Cornish mine engineer Richard Trevithick put the two together and made the first mine steam locomotive. In the 1820s, George Stephenson made better locomotives to pull a "train" of wagons carrying people, and the railways were born. We still have some steam trains, but there are now many other kinds. Some run deep in the subways under cities, others flash through the countryside faster than a racing car.

TAKING TO THE WATER

As steam engines were developed in the 1800s, they found their way into ships. Sailors didn't have to depend on the wind anymore. Then gasoline, diesel, and gas turbine engines were also put in ships. Today, we have a huge range of modern ships and boats, from racing sailboats and powerboats, to giant supertankers.

Train to the future?
Super-fast trains whisk people from one city to another at speeds of more than 125 mph (200 kph). The electric locomotives are reliable and don't cause much pollution. But transportation between small villages or towns needs more personal and adaptable vehicles than the ones that carry crowds between the big cities.

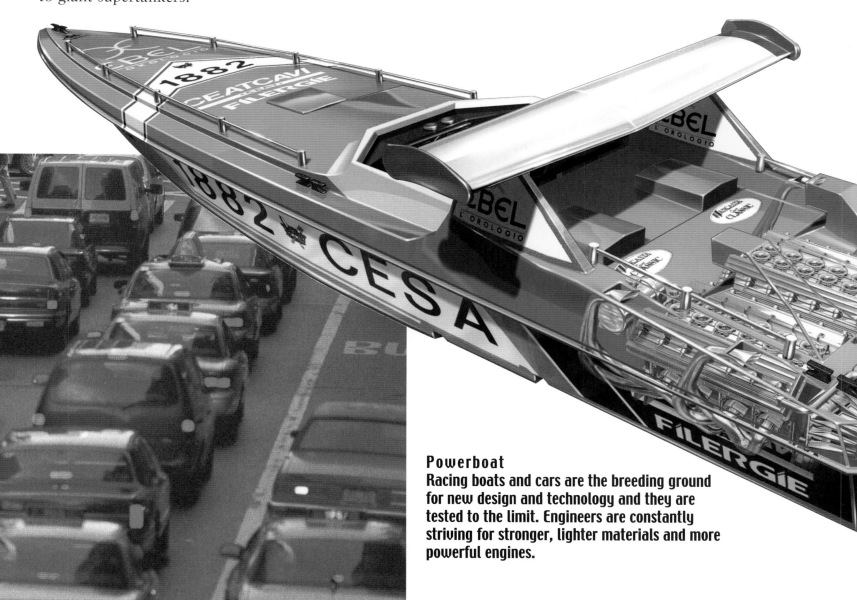

Powerboat
Racing boats and cars are the breeding ground for new design and technology and they are tested to the limit. Engineers are constantly striving for stronger, lighter materials and more powerful engines.

MOUNTAIN BIKE

Tread tires
The tires have a tread of small, pyramid-shaped blocks. These give good grip on soft ground, but they also allow soil and mud to slip off so they do not get stuck and harden in the tread.

Saddle height
The saddle stem tube that holds up the saddle can slide up and down inside the frame's down tube below, so the saddle height can be adjusted.

Frame
The frame is two triangles joined together for maximum strength with minimum materials and weight.

Frame tube
The walls of these tubes are not the same thickness all along. Shallow curves on the inside mean that the tube wall is thinner in the middle, where there is less stress, and thicker at the ends where the most bending strain occurs.

Rear changer
The rear changer has a caged jockey wheel that moves sideways to shift the chain from one cog to another. This bike has 7 rear cogs, which with the 3 front ones, gives a total of 21 gear combinations.

Front changer
The chain runs through a slot-shaped cage that moves sideways to shift it from one cog to another.

TYPES OF GEARS

Hub gears are contained in an extra-wide rear hub (the central part of the rear wheel.) They are changed by a chain that moves in and out of the hub from the side. The chain is worked by a cable attached to a trigger changer on the handlebars. Hub gears usually have only three or possibly five gear combinations.

Backpedal gears are also contained in the rear hub. There are two combinations, and you change from one to the other by pedaling backward slightly. In some designs, if you backpedal slightly more you apply the back hub brake.

Derailleur gears as shown here are exposed to rain, mud, and dirt. But they are easy to clean, adjust, and fix, and they give the widest variety of gear combinations.

Gear shifts

The gear shift levers, or buttons, are on the handlebars so the rider can change gear without letting go and losing control.

Safety feature

The handlebars are locked in position by a hex nut (also known as an Allen nut) in the top of their stem. The hex nut has a six-sided hole in it that is turned by inserting a six-sided hex wrench (Allen key). This design means there is no normal nut projecting at the top of the stem. A nut like that could cause injury if the rider slipped and fell onto it.

Handlebar height

The handlebar tube can slide up and down inside the frame tube below, to adjust the height of the handlebars. This is not only for different-sized riders, but also for riding position. Some people like to sit almost upright while others prefer a more crouched posture.

Brake blocks

The brake blocks are made of soft, sticky rubber so that they grip the wheel rim even if it's wet or muddy.

Dampers

The front forks (the two tubes that hold the front wheel) have damper suspension units. One design is a spring to absorb shocks and jolts, plus a pneumatic (air-filled) piston in a cylinder to restrain the spring's movements so that it doesn't keep bouncing up and down.

Serrated pedal grip

The pedals have serrated (toothed) edges at the front and back. These stick into the shoe's sole for a firm grip.

Quick-release clamp

This type of adjustable clamp is a combination of lever and also nut and bolt. It works fast and you don't need a wrench. You screw the nut by its arm to about half a turn before it gets really tight, then flip over the arm to fully tighten and lock it.

WHY HAVE GEARS?

Imagine a bicycle where you turn the pedals once and the rear wheel turns 10 times. This is a high gear. It's great for speeding downhill where you don't need to pedal a lot. But you couldn't press the pedals hard enough to turn them when going uphill.

Now imagine a bicycle where you turn the pedals once and the rear wheel turns less than once. This is a low gear. It's great for going up a steep slope, slowly but surely, and with not too much effort. However, you could never turn the pedals fast enough to pick up speed when going downhill.

Bicycles have gears for ease and convenience. You can adjust the speed and effort of pedaling to suit you. The bicycle then goes along according to the gearing, usually an average speed on the level, fast downhill, or slow uphill. Gears make cycling easier, but they don't change the total amount of effort you put in. Low gears make cycling uphill easier. But you are cycling slower and for longer, so your effort lasts longer.

RACING BIKE

No frame tubes
The frame is one piece of molded material called carbon fiber composite. It is extremely light and strong, shaped to withstand all the main stresses put on it without any excess material or weight.

No freewheel
If you stop pedaling on a sprint or racing bike, the pedals keep turning. There is no freewheel, like on a normal bike, that allows the pedals to keep still while the bicycle rolls along.

ON THE ROAD
Speed bicycles are too specialized to ride on roads. The basic design of the road racer, or touring bike, with its down-curved drop-handlebars, has not changed for more than 50 years.

No spokes
As a spoke moves through the air, both turning with the wheel and moving forward with it, this creates air resistance, or friction. The solid, spokeless wheel cuts out the air friction of the 30–40 normal spokes.

No air-filled tires
A cycle track is very flat, without lumps and bumps. So the speed or sprint bike needs only thin, solid rubber treads.

No left stays
The back wheel is fixed to one side of the frame—like the front wheel—for the same reason.

No pedal clips
Expert cyclists pull the pedal up as well as push it down, for greater power and speed. Older style pedals had clips and straps that fitted around a cycling shoe. Newer ones have clips that attach to clips on the soles of the shoes, similar to ski bindings that clip ski boots to skis.

BICYCLE SPEEDS
In a road race, a cyclist needs air-filled tires to iron out bumps in the road, gears to cope with the ups and downs of hills, and brakes to maneuver between competitors or avoid obstacles. But a cycle track is smooth and banked, usually indoors, empty aside from competitors, and exactly the same for every circuit. So the speed or sprint (short race) bicycle is the most stripped-down cycling machine available. Cyclists zoom along at 40mph (60kph) or more in races, with top speeds on specially-modified cycles of over 60mph (100kph).

Elbow rests
The rider rests her or his elbows on these "shelves" while gripping the handlebars above. The streamlined, torpedo-shaped ends keep the elbows from slipping off sideways.

No controls
There are no brakes or gears, so the handlebars look very bare. They face forward so the rider can crouch over them, hands at the front and forearms facing forward with elbows together. This is the best position for streamlined pedaling.

No gears
The moving parts of gear changers would add friction, weight, and wear to the cycle. The sizes of the two gear wheels, or cogs, front and back, are chosen by the rider at the start to fit his or her own cycling style, the track, the length of the race, the competition, and the conditions.

No brakes
There is rarely any need to brake on the special oval, banked cycle track. Brakes merely add more weight and air resistance and get in the way. The pedals can be used to slow the bike down by their fixed drive to the rear wheel.

No left fork
On a normal cycle, there are two tubes on either side of the front wheel in a Y shape, or fork. The sprint or speed cycle has only one, to cut air resistance. Like other forward-facing parts, it has a sharp leading edge and smooth sides for streamlining.

Not many spokes
The front wheel has three thin spokes. It does not have to be as strong as the rear wheel, which must transmit the turning force from the rear gear cog to the ground, so it can have less construction material.

HIGH GEARS

As you cycle along a level road on an ordinary bike, you push the pedals around once and the back wheel turns around about two times. But sprint and speed cycles have very high gear ratios or combinations. On a racing bike, one turn of the pedals turns the back wheel around four, five, or even more times!

TOURING BIKE

Rearview mirrors
Touring means riding long distances on the open road. Large rearview mirrors are vital for safety, to look behind for passing cars and bikes, or for emergency vehicles that need to get past.

Brake lever
This applies the front brake.

Accelerator twist grip
The speed of the engine is controlled by the accelerator twist grip, that is, by twisting the hand grip on the handlebar (usually the right one).

Cooling fins
A car has a cooling system with a radiator to take heat away from the engine. Most motorcycles do not. The cylinder, which is the part that gets hot because the fuel explodes inside it, has many metal flanges or fins. These pass excess heat to the air rushing past.

Fuel tank
The large fuel tank is just in front of the rider. It has a smooth curved top to cause minimum injury in case the rider slips onto it. It may have a map-holder on top, too.

Passenger seat
A second person can travel on the bike, on the second, or pillion, seat. The passenger should not try to lean or balance the bike. He or she should sit upright, grip the handhold-backrest justbehind, and act as "dead weight" to let the rider do the balancing.

Rider's seat
The well-rounded, padded seat is very comfortable for long journeys.

Saddlebags
A motorcycle has no trunk like a car, so luggage is stored in bags or cases called saddlebags. These are on frames, one on each side of the rear wheel. An equal weight of luggage on either side gives good balance.

Footrest
The passenger can rest his or her feet on flip-down footrests that fold back when not in use.

Rear brake
This is worked by a foot pedal on the right side of the bike. The foot pedal on the other side changes gears.

SPEED AND COMFORT

The freedom of the open road with the wind whistling past, the feeling of being part of the scenery, or snaking between cars to beat a traffic jam—motorcycle touring as an "easy rider" can be a lot of fun. But if it is very cold, raining, or icy, it is not so wonderful! The touring bike has a long wheelbase (distance between the wheels) that gives better roadholding and a smoother ride over bumps and holes than a short wheelbase. However, the long wheelbase is not so good for maneuvering around tight corners.

CYLINDERS AND STROKES

The motorcycle shown here is a transverse V twin. It has two cylinders, one on each side, at an angle to make a V-shape seen from the front. Two cylinders give a smoother ride and are more powerful than one.

There are many other designs. An in-line twin V has the cylinders one behind the other but still in a V shape, one pointing up and forward, and the other up and backward. There are also four-cylinder engines that are even smoother and more powerful, but also heavier and more complicated, with more to go wrong.

Many smaller off-road or dirt track motorcycles have just one cylinder. The engine may also be two-stroke. This means that the fuel ignites (explodes) and delivers power every two strokes, that is, every up and down stroke of the piston. Normal car and motorcycle engines are four-stroke.

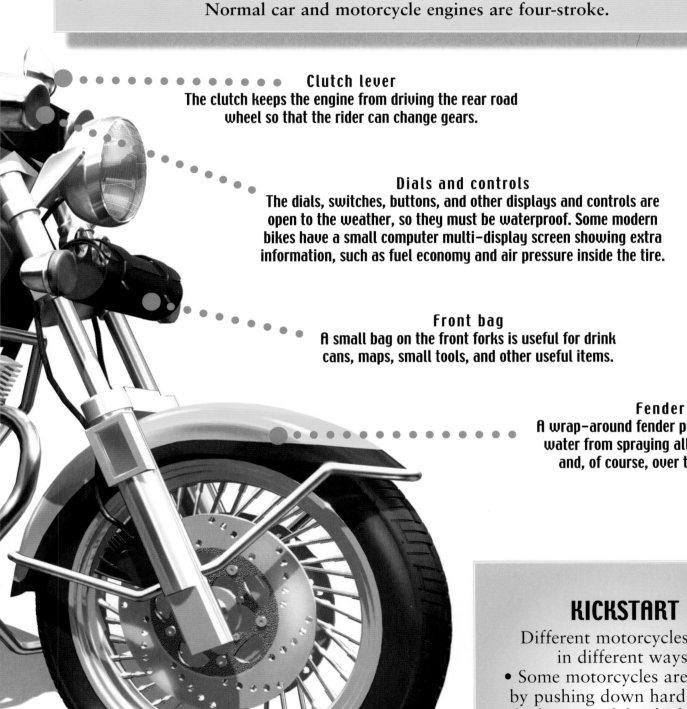

Clutch lever
The clutch keeps the engine from driving the rear road wheel so that the rider can change gears.

Dials and controls
The dials, switches, buttons, and other displays and controls are open to the weather, so they must be waterproof. Some modern bikes have a small computer multi-display screen showing extra information, such as fuel economy and air pressure inside the tire.

Front bag
A small bag on the front forks is useful for drink cans, maps, small tools, and other useful items.

Fender
A wrap-around fender prevents dirt and water from spraying all over the rider and, of course, over the machine.

KICKSTART

Different motorcycles start in different ways:

• Some motorcycles are started by pushing down hard on the kickstart pedal, which starts turning over the engine.

•Others have an electric motor, switched on by turning a key, like in a car, to start the engine.

SUPERBIKE

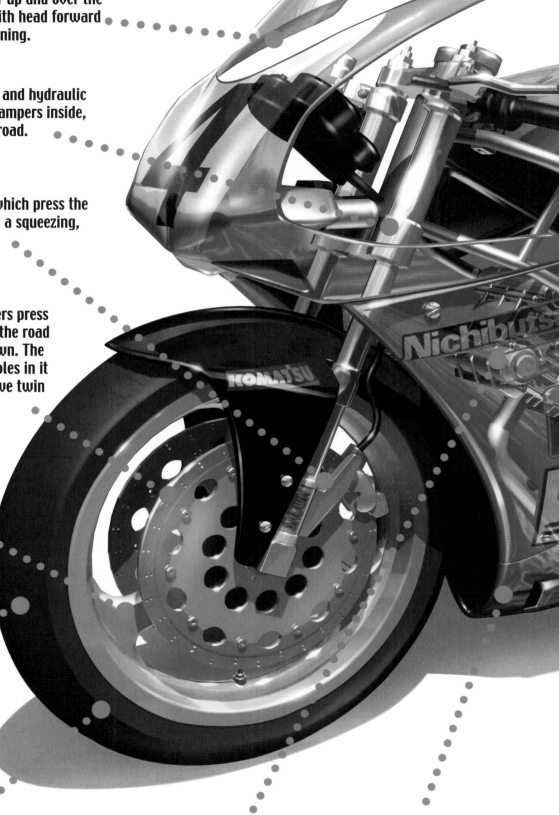

Windshield
The wind is very strong at more than 120mph (200kph). The windshield pushes the rushing air up and over the driver, who is also crouched down with head forward into the wind for streamlining.

Front suspension
The front forks are tubes with springs and hydraulic (oil-filled) or pneumatic (air-filled) dampers inside, to smooth out bumps in the road.

Brake calipers
The brake lever works the calipers, which press the brake pads onto the brake disc with a squeezing, scissorlike action.

Brake discs
The brake blocks, or pads, in the calipers press onto a large metal disc that is fixed to the road wheel and turns with it, to slow it down. The friction makes the disc hot so, it has holes in it for better cooling. Most superbikes have twin discs on the front wheel.

Few spokes
Many modern motorcycles do not have bicycle-type spokes in the wheels. The whole wheel is cast from one piece of metal alloy to make it strong but light. The lighter the wheel, the faster the engine can get it turning.

Slicks
Racetracks and fast roads are usually smooth and free of mud and dirt. So the superbike's tires, or slicks, do not need tread. They are just plain, soft, sticky rubber to grip the pavement.

Wraparound
The tire surface wraps around both sides. This allows the rider to lean over at an amazing angle to balance while going around corners at great speed, with the tire still gripping the road.

In-line twin V
This engine has two cylinders, one behind the other.

Fairings
A curved plastic or metal cover wraps around the main body of the motorcycle to cut down wind resistance.

POWER, WEIGHT, AND SPEED

The key to a fast vehicle is its power-to-weight ratio. This compares the weight of the vehicle with the amount of power that its engine produces to drive it along.

A superbike might weigh about 77lbs (170kg) and have an engine that produces 160 horsepower. A family car weighs up to 10 times as much and has an engine that is half as powerful. So its power-to-weight ratio is 20 times less! No wonder superbikes are among the fastest of all vehicles.

Low handlebars
The rider crouches low over the handlebars to minimize wind resistance.

Rider's seat
This is scooped out so that the driver sits as low as possible, hunched over the fuel tank for the least wind resistance.

Exhaust
Exhaust gases and fumes from each cylinder flow along pipes that come together into one pipe, and then pass through the silencer box before emerging into the air at the back, away from the rider and passenger.

Rear suspension
The rear wheel is at the end of a long leverlike arm called a swinging, or trailing, arm. This pivots with the main chassis just behind the engine. Large springs and hydraulic dampers smooth out bumps and vibrations.

Chain drive
Toothed cogs (sprockets, or gear wheels,) and a link chain, transfer turning power from the engine between the wheels to the rear wheel. Some bikes have a spinning driveshaft instead of a chain.

Gear pedal
The rider changes gear with a foot pedal by flicking it up and down. The foot pedal on the other side applies the rear brake.

HOW MANY CCS?

A cc is a measure of volume. One cc is one cubic centimeter, that is, a cube roughly the size of a lump of sugar. Motorcycles, cars, and other vehicles have engines measured in ccs or liters (one liter is 1,000 ccs). The volume that's measured is the amount of air pushed aside as the pistons move the full distance inside their cylinders.

- A small moped or track motorcycle is 50 ccs.
- A small racing motorcycle is up to 250 ccs.
- A medium motorcycle is 500 ccs.
- A large motorcycle is 750 or 900 ccs.
- There are also superbikes of 1,000 ccs (one liter) and more!
- A small family car might have an engine size of 900–1,000 ccs (up to one liter).
- Big luxury cars are 2.5 liters or more.

FAMILY CAR

Rear wheel drive
Most ordinary family cars are rear wheel drive, where the engine turns only the two roadwheels at the back. This gives the best combination of balance, roadholding, steering, and handling. Some smaller cars are front wheel drive, but the extra parts needed to turn and steer the front wheels mean extra weight and wear.

Spare wheel and tire
The spare wheel is usually under one side of the rear of the car next to the fuel tank. If the trunk is full, everything must be taken out to change the wheel.

Air bag
In case of a sudden shock or stop, a plastic bag bursts from a container in front of the driver (usually in the middle of the steering wheel) and begins to blow itself up with gas, all in less than one-tenth of a second.

Rear suspension
Springs and hydraulic dampers (pistons in oil-filled cylinders) allow the car body to sway smoothly as the air-filled tires and the wheels absorb vibrations, bumps, and jolts from the road beneath.

Fuel tank
The tank is usually under one side of the rear of the car next to the spare wheel. In this position, the fuel is farthest from the hot engine and least likely to catch fire in an accident.

Differential box
This allows the two rear wheels to be turned by the engine at different speeds while going around corners.

CAT
The exhaust fumes and gases are made safer by a CAT, or catalytic convertor. This absorbs and keeps back some of the most dangerous exhaust products.

SMART CARS

More and more cars come with electronic gadgets, sensors, and microchips. In the engine, they monitor how much fuel is being used and help the driver to be more economical. They keep check on the levels of various fluids, such as gasoline or diesel, engine oil, gearbox oil, braking system fluid, and hydraulic oil, cooling fluid and even windshield-washer fluid! They also track engine temperature and oil pressure, and warn when replacements will be needed for brakes and other wearing parts.

A satellite navigation unit using the GPS (global positioning system) can pinpoint the car's position to within a few yards on a local map stored in electronic memory and display this on a screen. Radio and radar links to speed-warning signs tell the driver about exceeding the speed limit. A carphone provides a link to the outside world.

ABS

The automatic braking system (ABS) stops a car from skidding. Without ABS, brakes suddenly slammed on could lock, so the wheel stops turning but the car continues on in a skid. With no grip on the road it's difficult to bring the vehicle to a controlled stop. With ABS, sensors in the wheels react if the brakes are about to lock, and brake pressure is released slightly. This means that the wheel keeps turning and the tire holds its grip on the road while being slowed down. ABS kicks in several times each second, making a rattling noise. The result is a fast, safe, controlled, non-skid stop.

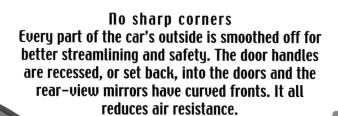

No sharp corners
Every part of the car's outside is smoothed off for better streamlining and safety. The door handles are recessed, or set back, into the doors and the rear-view mirrors have curved fronts. It all reduces air resistance.

Prop shaft
The engine turns gears in the gearbox and these turn the propeller or prop shaft. It runs along the underside of the car to the differential box between the rear wheels.

Front suspension
This has springs and dampers like the rear suspension. The steering parts are also pivoted so they can tilt as the wheels bob up and down in relation to the engine.

Engine
Most family cars have four-cylinder gasoline engines. The modern engine is about twice as efficient and clean as an engine of 30 years ago. That means it gets twice as much power out of the same amount of fuel and produces only half the amount of harmful exhaust fumes.

Exhaust recycling
Exhaust gases from the engine are sent around again so that the unburned fuel in them can be used more effectively.

Steering mechanism
The steering wheel turns a rod that has a small gear cog or pinion at its base. The teeth of the cog sit in a straight row of teeth known as the rack along another rod whose ends connect to each front wheel. This is known as rack-and-pinion steering.

WHAT'S THE DIFFERENCE?

The differential allows two wheels on either side of a car to rotate at different speeds while still being driven by the engine. Why? Imagine a car turning left. The wheel on the right covers a longer curve or arc than the left one, but during the same time. So it must turn faster to travel the extra distance. If both wheels are being driven at the same speed they lose grip and "skip" or "hop" so they can cover their different distances.

The differential allows this to happen. As the wheel on the outside of the corner turns faster, the one on the inside turns more slowly by the same amount. This gives smooth cornering. Nearly all cars and trucks have this system.

F1 RACECAR

Front wing
Specially-shaped to produce a force that presses the car down onto the track.

Radio antenna
The driver and his racing team can keep in contact by radio.

Tire
F1 tires are wide and have hardly any tread. Tires for use in the wet have more tread. During a race, the tires can heat up to 230°F (110°C).

Wheel
Each wheel is held in place by a single screw-on wheelnut, which can be removed very quickly. This is so that the wheels and tires can be changed rapidly during a race.

Steering wheel
The small steering wheel is fitted with buttons and switches that enable the driver to change gear and do many other things without having to let go of the wheel.

Cockpit
The driver's cockpit is very cramped, with almost no room to move. It is so small that the driver must remove the steering wheel before he gets in or out.

Sponsor's name
Running an F1 racing team is incredibly expensive. Most of the money comes from sponsors, who pay the team to advertise their names on the cars.

Fuel tanks
The tanks on either side of the driver have a honeycomblike mesh inside. This keeps the fuel from splashing around too fast inside, which would upset the car's delicate balance.

Driver's survival cell
The driver lies in a tube-shaped survival cell or "cocoon" made of extremely strong but light composite material, with only the head and arms exposed. The cell resists breaking in a crash to protect the driver.

THE CHAMPIONSHIP MACHINE

The Formula 1 racecar can accelerate from 0–100mph (0–160kph) and brake back to a standstill, all in less than six seconds. For this, the driver only needs the first and second gears out of the six usually fitted. The fastest speeds are over 200mph (320kph). A Formula 1 race is usually about 200mi (300km) and takes up to two hours. Every aspect of the car, including steering angle and fuel tank size, is reset for each racetrack. Dozens of sensors inside the car radio send information on every aspect of its performance back to the team in the pits. This information transfer is known as telemetry. The team can then advise the driver on the return radio link.

CARS WITH WINGS

Just as the wings of a plane lift it upward into the air, the wings on an F1 car push it down onto the track. This is because of their shape. On a plane, the top of the wing is curved and the underside is flat, which means that the air presses less on the top than on the bottom, so the wing is pushed upward. F1 car wings are mounted the other way up, so that the force pushes them downward. This helps the car to grip without slowing it down too much, and gives the driver more control when cornering. The wings and the body shape produce so much force that at 150mph (240kph) the car could race upside-down on a ceiling without falling off!

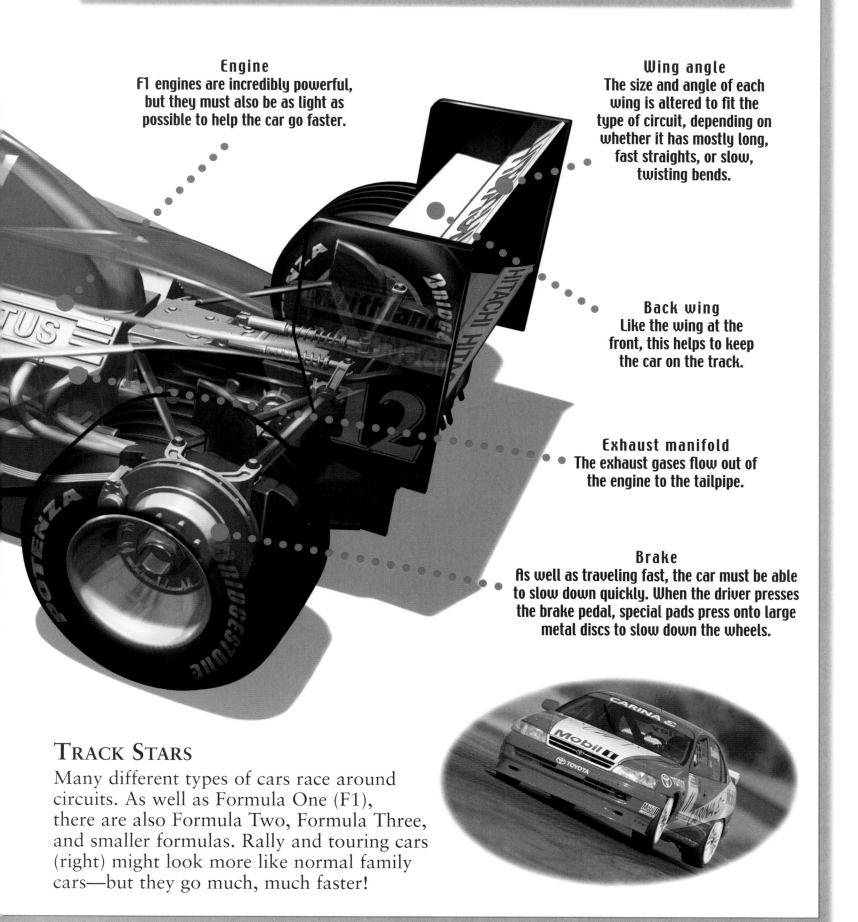

Engine
F1 engines are incredibly powerful, but they must also be as light as possible to help the car go faster.

Wing angle
The size and angle of each wing is altered to fit the type of circuit, depending on whether it has mostly long, fast straights, or slow, twisting bends.

Back wing
Like the wing at the front, this helps to keep the car on the track.

Exhaust manifold
The exhaust gases flow out of the engine to the tailpipe.

Brake
As well as traveling fast, the car must be able to slow down quickly. When the driver presses the brake pedal, special pads press onto large metal discs to slow down the wheels.

TRACK STARS

Many different types of cars race around circuits. As well as Formula One (F1), there are also Formula Two, Formula Three, and smaller formulas. Rally and touring cars (right) might look more like normal family cars—but they go much, much faster!

STRETCH LIMOUSINE

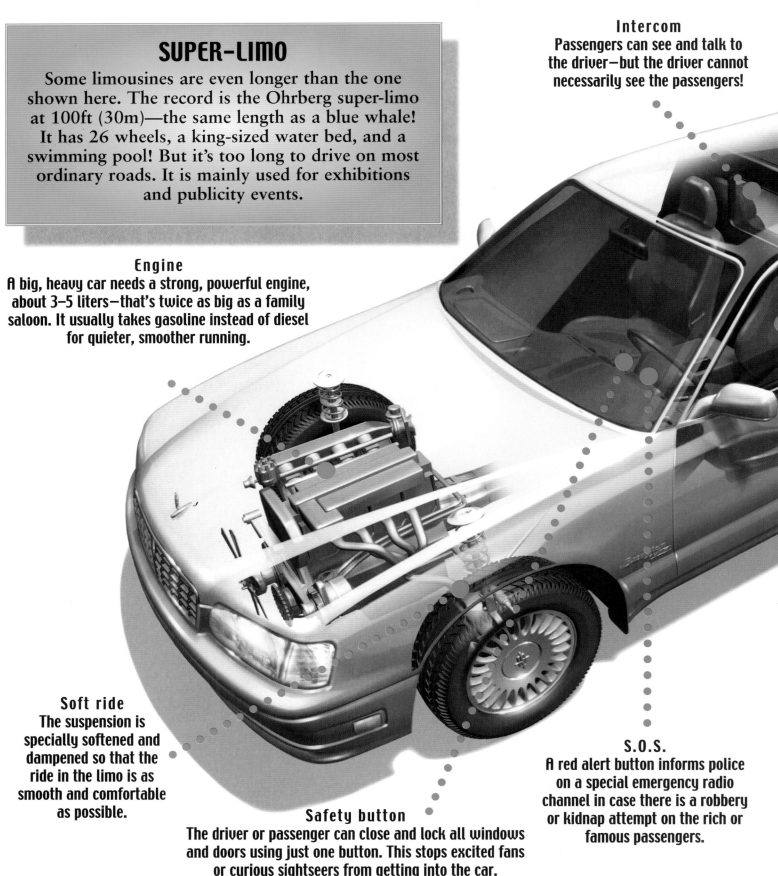

SUPER-LIMO

Some limousines are even longer than the one shown here. The record is the Ohrberg super-limo at 100ft (30m)—the same length as a blue whale! It has 26 wheels, a king-sized water bed, and a swimming pool! But it's too long to drive on most ordinary roads. It is mainly used for exhibitions and publicity events.

Intercom
Passengers can see and talk to the driver—but the driver cannot necessarily see the passengers!

Engine
A big, heavy car needs a strong, powerful engine, about 3–5 liters—that's twice as big as a family saloon. It usually takes gasoline instead of diesel for quieter, smoother running.

Soft ride
The suspension is specially softened and dampened so that the ride in the limo is as smooth and comfortable as possible.

S.O.S.
A red alert button informs police on a special emergency radio channel in case there is a robbery or kidnap attempt on the rich or famous passengers.

Safety button
The driver or passenger can close and lock all windows and doors using just one button. This stops excited fans or curious sightseers from getting into the car.

THE STRETCHED PART

Originally the "stretch" limousine was made by taking an existing luxury car, cutting it in half and welding extra panels into the gaps to make it longer. Then a new top-class interior was fitted with leather seats, luxurious carpets, and all the trimmings. Today, various specialized vehicle-makers build limos exactly to the owner's specifications. Some have fold-out beds so that they can become a luxury hotel on wheels!

Office on the move
On long trips, the limo can be a place to work. It can be fitted with a computer linked to the Internet, and a VCR so that movie or music star passengers can watch their latest movies or videos.

Radio links
Various antennae send and receive signals for radio, TV, telephone, Internet, and also private encrypted (secrecy-coded) radio and walkie-talkie channels.

Tinted windows
The windows of the passenger compartment are tinted and have a reflective coating. People trying to see in from the outside can only see their own faces. The windows are often bulletproof, too.

Comforts of home
The limo has a carphone, a TV (with satellite, of course), a sound system, a bar, hot drinks, and many other comforts.

Expert driver
The driver, or chauffeur, must be specially-trained not only to drive safely and within the law, but also to start and stop very smoothly and to guide the long limo around awkward turns and avoid sharp corners.

Keeping cool and quiet
Air-conditioning and heating keeps passengers cool when it is hot and warm in cold weather. It also filters out the smoke and fumes from traffic jams. Special body panels and thick windows keep out the noise.

WHO BUYS A STRETCH LIMO?

Whoever wants one and has enough money! However, it is a very expensive "toy" to leave sitting in the garage. And it may not get through the barrier at the local supermarket car park. This is why 9 out of 10 large limousines are owned by vehicle rental companies. A limo can be rented by the hour, day, week, or longer. The driver costs extra, too. Big limos are hired for film and music stars, bosses of big companies, royalty, presidents, politicians, and public figures—and ordinary people who decide to splash out on a special day—like a wedding.

4X4-FOUR-WHEEL DRIVE

Silencer
This box in the exhaust pipe makes the waste gases and fumes from the engine slower and quieter. It may also contain a CAT (catalytic convertor) with special substances that remove some of the most dangerous chemicals in the fumes.

ATTs
All terrain tires have thicker, chunkier tread than normal road tires. They give good all-purpose grip on a variety of surfaces, from highways to plowed fields.

Chassis
Steel box girders make the car's chassis, or framework, very strong and rigid, so that it can take knocks from rocks and potholes.

Rear door
Some rear doors are hinged to the roof so they lift up in one piece. Others are horizontal two-part so the window section folds up and the lower part hinges down to form a tailgate platform. Others are vertical two-part, hinged at each side so they open in the middle.

Rear drive
The rear drive, or half shafts, turn the rear road wheels when the vehicle is in RWD or 4WD mode.

Light cages
If a 4x4 is used off-road it may skid and bump into trees, posts, and other objects. Wire cages around the lights prevent their coverings and bulbs from being smashed. It's easier to straighten out the wire cage than to replace the bulb and cover.

Limited slip diff
This box of gear cogs stops the vehicle from getting bogged down in slippery mud.

Suspension
4x4s have strong, stiff suspension to cope with bumps and holes on rough ground and also with the heavy loads they may carry.

Prop shaft
The propeller shaft carries the turning force from the engine back to the rear road wheels.

WHY 4WD?

A normal family car is 2WD or two-wheel drive—only two of the road wheels are turned by the engine. In small cars, it may be the front two (FWD), in larger ones it's the rear two (RWD). In a 4WD (four-wheel drive) vehicle all four road wheels are made to turn by the engine. This allows much more power to get through to the road, giving improved grip or traction. The vehicle has a better grip on slippery mud and ice, and more control in going up and down very steep hills and getting out of potholes or over rocks and roots. It also allows heavier loads to be carried.

However, 4WD uses up much more fuel. This is because the engine has to turn and work an extra set of road wheel drive parts. So most 4WDs have a lever or button that switches to 2WD for smooth roads, to save fuel—and wear and tear.

Head restraint
As a 4x4 travels over rough ground, the passengers bump and move around. Shaped restraints help to steady their heads so that they can avoid neck pain and whiplash injuries.

Engine
Most 4x4s have diesel engines. They may be heavier and noisier than gasoline engines, but they are usually more reliable and also need less servicing and maintenance.

Drive control
The driver uses a stickshift to change between FWD, RWD, and 4WD.

Front drive
The front drive shafts turn the front road wheels when the vehicle is in FWD or 4WD mode.

Disc brakes
A big, heavy car like a 4x4 needs strong brakes, so it is equipped with disc brakes all around. These are power-assisted, which means that the driver's pressure on the foot pedal is boosted by hydraulic pressure supplied by the engine.

EVEN MORE GRIP

Four wheels turning may not be enough in very slippery conditions like ice and snow. So special snow chains are wrapped around the tires to give even more grip.

LIMITED SLIP DIFF

In a 2WD vehicle, the wheels on either side of the axle can rotate at different speeds while still being driven by the engine. This is called the diff or differential. It can cause trouble when off-road. Imagine the left back wheel of the car is in a very slippery place, such as on ice. It has hardly anything to grip, so it can spin almost freely. The diff allows it to do this, while the right back wheel—which is on dry pavement and can grip—simply keeps still. The vehicle is stuck! This doesn't happen when a vehicle has limited or non-slip diff. Only a limited difference is allowed between the speeds of the two wheels. Beyond this the drive is still applied to the slower wheel, which hauls the vehicle out of the rut, so it's no longer stuck.

PICKUP TRUCK

Turbo diesel
The turbocharged diesel engine has about twice the power of an ordinary family car engine.

Winch
This is a cable wound onto a reel or drum, with a hook or link on the end. The drum spins easily one way so that the cable can be unwound. Then the drum turns slowly but powerfully to wind it back in. If the pickup is parked, the winch can haul items toward it. If the pickup cannot climb a steep hill, the cable can be unwound and attached to something higher up, like a tree, pole, or building. Then the winch turns to pull up the pickup!

Bull bar
There aren't usually many real bulls to push out of the way. The bull bar is really a large front bumper for pushing branches and other items aside, or to protect the pickup in case of a crash.

Clean headlights
Because pickups often travel over soft ground and unpaved roads, they get covered in mud. The headlights have their own water sprayers and wipers to keep them clean.

Stiff suspension
The pickup's suspension springs and dampers are very stiff. That is, they do not soften the ride very much. This is because pickups are built to carry heavy loads over rough grounds, where soft suspension might strain or break.

Ground clearance
All parts on the underside of the pickup are well above the ground. This is called high ground clearance and prevents damage as the vehicle goes over rocks and roots. There may also be sheets of metal covering the undersides of more fragile parts.

4WD
Most pickups have four-wheel drive where the engine turns all four road wheels.

THE WORKING PICKUP

Pickups were specially-designed as work vehicles for people to carry various large and awkward loads on short trips. They can "pick up" almost anything. They are used by construction workers, farmers, maintenance engineers, mechanics, foresters, park rangers, and many other people. The loads can vary from bricks to pieces of wood, tools such as shovels and sledgehammers, concrete mixers, sand and rocks, and chickens and other farm animals. Most pickups have hooks, cleats, or similar anchor points around the load bay so that the load can be tied or strapped down safely. Some have covers that can be tied over the load bay to protect the contents from rain and snow.

Spotlights
The roof spots can be tilted and swivelled to light up areas around the vehicle. Pickups often work in the dark, rescuing farm animals or attending breakdowns.

Roll bar
If the pickup accidentally rolls over onto its top side, the large U-shaped roll bar holds the cabin off the ground so that the people inside stay safe.

Spare wheel
The spare wheel is not hidden in the trunk or underneath like in ordinary cars. It is attached to the rear tailgate and ready for action. In this position, it also works as an extra rear rubber bumper.

Load bay
The pickup's great advantage is its open load area. Almost anything can be thrown in and easily taken out again.

Side step
Because of the extra-large wheels the pickup's door may be 3ft (1m) above the ground. So you climb in using the side step about half-way up.

Sprung seat
Because pickups are built for rough ground and have stiff suspension, the seats have extra springs and padding so that the driver and passenger are not shaken to pieces.

Side exhaust
Ordinary cars have their exhaust pipes and boxes along the underside. But the pickup has them along the sides as part of its high ground clearance for rough terrain.

TYPES OF PICKUP

Pickups are popular in every part of the country. Some pickups have a longer cab so that two or three people can sit on the rear seat behind the driver and front passenger. The flatbed pickup has a load bay with fold-down sides or no sides at all, so heavy loads can be slid on and off the load platform. The crane pickup has a small crane and a winch at the back to retrieve broken-down cars.

COMBINE HARVESTER

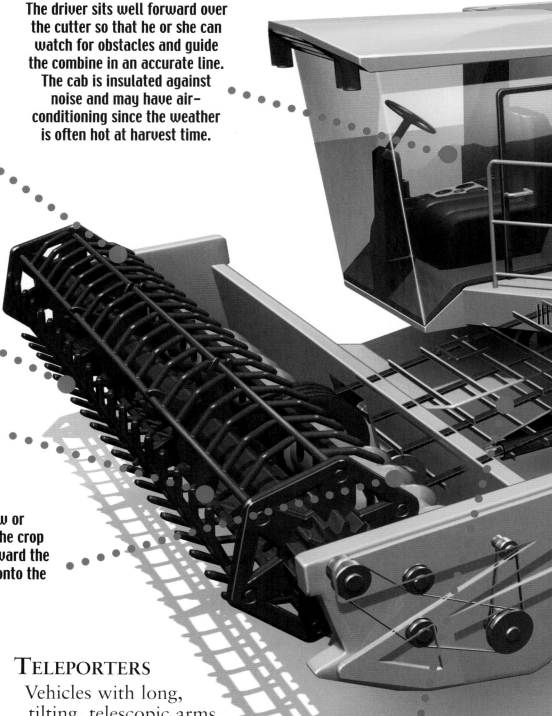

Rotating reel
The large reel at the front pulls the crop down and back, toward and over the cutter bar. Guide pegs at each end help the driver to steer the combine so that no strip of crop is left unharvested.

Cab
The driver sits well forward over the cutter so that he or she can watch for obstacles and guide the combine in an accurate line. The cab is insulated against noise and may have air-conditioning since the weather is often hot at harvest time.

Lifters
Sometimes heavy rain knocks the crops over and flattens them to the ground. The lifters slide under them like the prongs of forks so that they are harvested instead of going underneath the cutter.

Cutter bar
This slices the stalks of the crops almost at ground level. The height of the cutter can be adjusted for harvesting different plants.

Crop auger
An auger is a large screw or corkscrew-shaped blade. The crop auger pulls the cut crops toward the middle of the machine and onto the feeder elevator.

TELEPORTERS
Vehicles with long, tilting, telescopic arms can carry loads and lift them into difficult-to-reach places.

Feeder elevator
A continually-moving conveyor belt carries the cut crops from the front into the body of the combine.

MANY JOBS IN ONE

The combine harvester is named after the fact that it combines, or joins, all the jobs normally done when harvesting grain crops, such as wheat, barley, oats, and rye. The first combines appeared in the U.S. in the 1920s, towed and powered by tractors. Self-propelled combines with their own engines became popular in the 1950s. Modern combines have a range of cutting heads, bars, and reels to suit different crops, including beans, sweetcorn, and sorghum. Each one does the work of up to 100 people using hand-harvesting tools.

Engine
A large diesel engine drives the combine's main wheels and also powers the many moving parts, belts, screws, augers, and shakers inside the vehicle.

Grain tank
Grain is stored here until the tank is full, or it can be blown or conveyed into a truck or trailer that is driven alongside the combine as it crawls across the field.

Baler
A baling attachment can be fitted to the rear of the combine. It presses the straw into cylinder-shaped bales and ties them with twine.

Straw walker or shaker
The shaker rattles back and forth and shakes the straw (stalks) toward the rear. Grain and other material fall through the sieve onto the grain pan. Another corkscrewlike auger lifts the threshed, clean grains up into the main storage tank.

Grain pan
The grain is carried backward and powerful blasts of air from the chaff fan blow the lighter pieces (chaff) upward away from it.

Drive wheels
The large wheels under the main part of the machine push the combine along. Smaller wheels at the rear steer the vehicle.

Threshing cylinder
The thresher turns around and shakes the crop so violently that the grain falls away from the seed cases, stalks, leaves, and other unwanted pieces.

COMPUTERIZED COMBINES

Remote-sensing satellites high above in space can survey huge expanses of a farm's fields that would take a long time to check on the ground, and beam pictures of the fields down by radio. The farmer can tell by the different computer-enhanced colors which areas of crop might be diseased or in need of pesticides, fertilizers, or other sprays, and which are ready to harvest. This information, plus the size and shape of the area to be cut, are fed into the combine's on-board computer. The computer works out the best route for harvesting the field. It can also avoid any poor areas that are not worth cutting. The route is displayed on a screen for the driver to follow.

FRONT-LOADER

Lights
To get the job done on time, the front-loader and driver may have to work nights. The lights move with the bucket so it is always brightly lit. There are also lights at the rear, and the driver's seat swivels around, too, because a front-loader spends plenty of time in reverse.

Hydraulic hoses
High-pressure oil is pumped along these flexible pipes into the cylinders to work the rams. The pipes bend so that the front-loader booms and bucket can move. They have steel mesh inside their walls for extra strength.

Bucket tilt rams
The bucket tilts up or down when these hydraulic rods and pistons push or pull on it.

"Artic"
The front-loader is articulated—it has a hinge or joint in the middle. It steers not by twisting the wheels, but by moving the whole front end, including the bucket, to one side or the other.

Bucket
An average bucket is 7 or 8ft (2.5–3m) wide. It is not always full of earth or rocks. The front-loader can be used to carry loads, such as bags of cement or blocks of bricks, around the site.

SWL
Most construction machines have SWLs, safe working loads. A front-loader may have a SWL of 7–8 tons for a bucket.

Main booms
These link the front-loader body to the bucket. They are moved by hydraulic rams.

Raise-lower rams
This pair of hydraulic rods and pistons pushes the booms and raises the bucket more than 8ft (3m) into the air, so it can tip its contents into a dump truck or earthmover.

BUCKETS OF BUCKETS
The bucket shown here is a typical all-purpose design for gouging into and lifting soil, earth, small rocks, gravel, and sand. There are many other bucket designs for different jobs. A smoothing bucket is lower and wider to scrape a large area level. A basket bucket is made of steel bars like a cage for lifting lighter, looser material such as hay, straw, and household refuse.

Cab
The driver sits in an air-conditioned, vibration-proofed, and sound-proofed cab. This protects the driver from being deafened and shaken up by a day's work.

Controls
Hand levers or buttons control the bucket's movements. Floor pedals and the steering wheel make the whole front-loader move around.

Engine
A heavy-duty diesel engine provides the power for turning the wheels, and for the hydraulic system to raise and lower the bucket. The engine produces about 180–200 horsepower (almost three times the power of a small family car).

Huge tires
A big front-loader has tires taller than the average adult. They have deep tread to grip soft ground. Sometimes they are filled partly with water for extra weight and grip.

FRONT-LOADERS GALORE
Front-loaders, excavators, and other load-movers find jobs in all kinds of work, from piling up scrapped cars, to scooping up gravel and sand for building, to scraping up sea salt from shallow coastal lagoons.

IT'S ALL DONE BY HYDRAULICS

Many large vehicles and machines rely on hydraulic systems. They use oil under very high pressure. It is pumped along a pipe or hose into a large metal tube-shaped cylinder. Closely fitting inside the cylinder is a rod-shaped piston. As the oil is forced into the cylinder it pushes the piston in front of it. The piston usually has a long metal rod attached to it, and the other end is linked to the part that moves. The pressure is so great that if a hose sprang a leak, the thin jet of oil spurting out of it would blast a small hole straight through the body of a person standing in the way.

Like our own muscles, hydraulic pistons can only push. For two-way movement there are two pistons that rock the part to be moved like a seesaw. Or two pistons face each other in the same long cylinder, and the oil is pumped from one end of the cylinder to the other. This gives push-pull power.

BULLDOZER

Blade controls
These levers control the hydraulic rams to raise or lower the blade and to tilt it up or down.

Bulldozer controls
There are few controls for the bulldozer itself. The main ones are two levers that make the tracks work on each side. The bulldozer has no steering wheel. It turns by slowing or stopping the track on one side while the other track still runs, making the bulldozer swing around at its middle.

Track drive
The main cog, or sprocket, wheel is driven by the engine to make the track run. On some bulldozers, there is a front drive cog, too, and possibly repeater cogs along the length of the track.

Track
The track is the caterpillar, or crawler, track—an endless loop of plates joined by pins.

Hydraulic array
The engine supplies the main hydraulic power to the cab, in the form of oil at very high pressure in a pipe. This is divided into many pipes, each with its own control, that send oil to work the various hydraulic rams and systems.

Track pin
Pins link the track plates to each other. If one plate gets bent or broken, the pins can be taken out and a new plate can then be inserted.

Track plate
Some tracks have plates made of very hard and strong rubber, others of metal. The ridge across the track jabs into the ground to give amazing grip.

WHY THE NAME?

The name is a version of the term "bull dose." This was a dose of sedative given to a bull, which was more powerful than that needed by a smaller, calmer cow. So giving a "dose fit for a bull" meant giving an extra-powerful, or very strong, amount of something. It fits the bulldozer's huge size and mighty power.

WHAT DO BULLDOZERS DO?

They are designed to push, scrape, and level rough ground, and to move piles of rocks, earth, gravel, sand, and other loose material. But they can do much more—

- A bulldozer can drive through an area of scrubs, young trees, or rough ground, flattening everything in its path.

- It can attach a cable or chain to bigger trees and pull them out of the ground, or drag over walls and pylons.

- Two bulldozers with a long steel cable strung between them can drive either side of a wooden or weak brick building and make it topple to the ground.

- A bulldozer can also push and move heavy items, such as large steel pipes.

- The bulldozer can rescue other vehicles if they get stuck by dragging them out of ditches or mud onto solid ground.

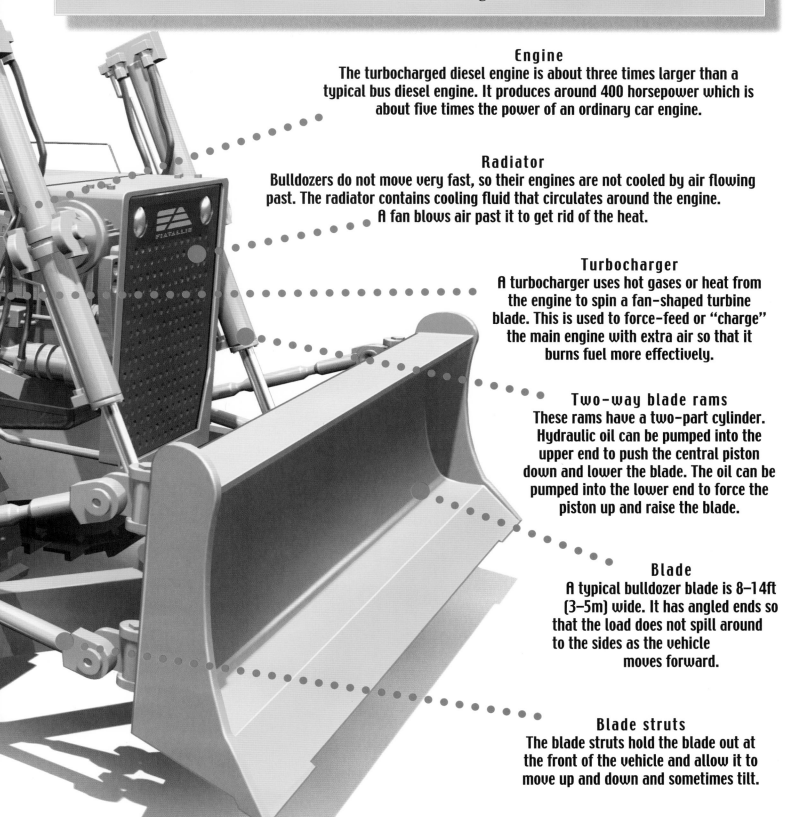

Engine
The turbocharged diesel engine is about three times larger than a typical bus diesel engine. It produces around 400 horsepower which is about five times the power of an ordinary car engine.

Radiator
Bulldozers do not move very fast, so their engines are not cooled by air flowing past. The radiator contains cooling fluid that circulates around the engine. A fan blows air past it to get rid of the heat.

Turbocharger
A turbocharger uses hot gases or heat from the engine to spin a fan-shaped turbine blade. This is used to force-feed or "charge" the main engine with extra air so that it burns fuel more effectively.

Two-way blade rams
These rams have a two-part cylinder. Hydraulic oil can be pumped into the upper end to push the central piston down and lower the blade. The oil can be pumped into the lower end to force the piston up and raise the blade.

Blade
A typical bulldozer blade is 8–14ft (3–5m) wide. It has angled ends so that the load does not spill around to the sides as the vehicle moves forward.

Blade struts
The blade struts hold the blade out at the front of the vehicle and allow it to move up and down and sometimes tilt.

FLATBED SEMI

Suspension
The extremely strong suspension has a trailing, or swinging, arm design.

Securing the load
Before the flatbed semi goes, this front-loader will be secured or tied down tightly with chains and very strong straps. Moveable parts like the bucket must also be secured in case they come loose or swing around.

Trailer unit
The trailer receives its electricity and its hydraulic power to work the brakes, suspension, and other systems from the tractor unit through flexible wires and hoses.

Flashing lights
The yellow flashing lights warn other drivers and road users that the vehicle and its load are very large.

WIDE LOAD

Wide load
Vehicles over a certain width must have clear signs saying so. The sign warns other drivers that it may be difficult to pass since the flatbed semi may be wider than one of the lanes on the highway.

Multi-wheels
As many as 20 or more wheels spread the huge weight of the load. The front-loader on this flatbed semi may weigh 20 tons.

THE WEIGHT PROBLEM

The flatbed semi may arrive at a weak bridge, a steep hill, a railroad crossing, or a similar place where its huge weight could cause problems. The weight must be taken into consideration to decide if it is safe to continue.

- MGW or maximum gross weight is the weight of the whole thing—tractor unit, trailer unit, load, fuel, even the driver's sandwiches!

- Axle weight depends on how many axles there are, that is, sets of wheels. The more axles and wheels, the better the weight is spread over a larger area.

- Payload is the weight of just the load, without the flatbed semi.

GIANTS ON THE HIGHWAY

Huge transporters, wide loads, eighteen-wheelers, and convoys roar down the highway, carrying every kind of cargo from car parts and washing machines to beds, flowers, and chocolate.

Bend in the middle
The articulated joint or link between the tractor and trailer units allows the whole vehicle to bend in the middle, for going around corners more easily.

Tractor unit
The truck at the front is the tractor unit. In this case "tractor" just means something that pulls.

Drive wheels
The trailer's wheels are not turned by the engine. Only the wheels on the truck or tractor unit are driven by the engine.

Low load
The load is carried on a low platform slung between the sets of wheels at the front and rear. The lower it is, the more stable it is, and less likely to sway or topple because of a bumpy road or sudden corner.

Ramps
Strong metal ramps are stored under the trailer. They are brought out and attached to the back so that loads can be rolled or dragged onto the platform.

Winch and cable
The trailer has a large winch at the front. This winds a steel cable onto a drum slowly and with tremendous power. The winch is used for hauling loads onto the trailer.

PLANNING THE ROUTE

Driving a giant flatbed semi is very different from driving a car! The driver may have to tell the police and other authorities about his or her journey, especially if the load may be dangerous, as with drums of chemicals. The driver must plan the route carefully in advance to avoid problems such as—

- Sharp corners.
- Weak bridges.
- Low bridges, cables, and other places where there is limited height or headroom.
- Places where the ground is soft and may subside (sink or collapse).
- Places where the road surface is bumpy.
- Roads or openings with restricted width such as gateways and driveways.

EIGHTEEN-WHEELER

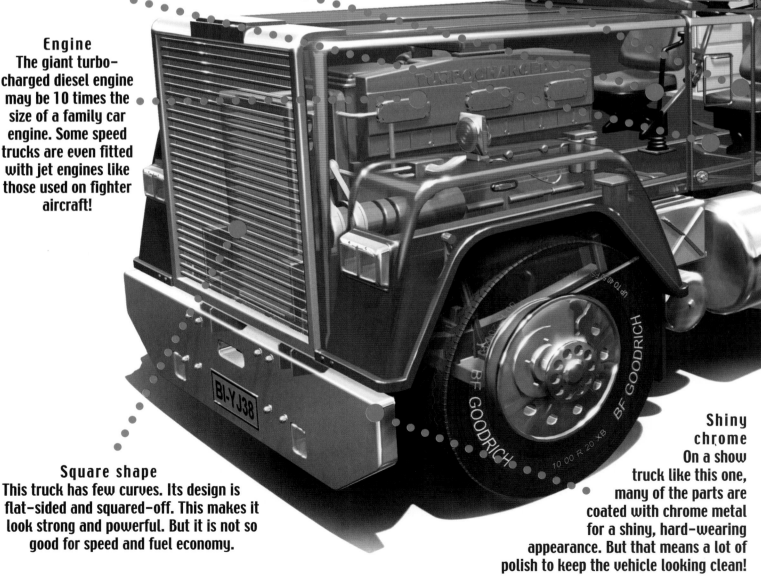

Air horns
Compressed air blasts out of the horns to make a sound heard more than 1mi (2km) away.

Cockpit
There are lots of dials and controls. The dashboard looks more like a plane cockpit or flight deck.

CB radio
Drivers keep in touch with each other by CB, or citizen's band radio. They talk and pass the time, discuss the weather and road conditions, or their trucks and loads, and warn each other of traffic jams or accidents.

Gears
There may be 10, 12, or more gears to help the truck pull away uphill with its 40-ton load, or cruise down the highway at its maximum speed.

Driver's seat
The driver's seat is reinforced and strengthened with a pilotlike safety harness for a seat belt to cope with the amazing acceleration and cornering speed.

Limiter
Working trucks are fitted with speed limiters since in many countries they are not allowed to go as fast as ordinary cars.

Engine
The giant turbocharged diesel engine may be 10 times the size of a family car engine. Some speed trucks are even fitted with jet engines like those used on fighter aircraft!

Square shape
This truck has few curves. Its design is flat-sided and squared-off. This makes it look strong and powerful. But it is not so good for speed and fuel economy.

Shiny chrome
On a show truck like this one, many of the parts are coated with chrome metal for a shiny, hard-wearing appearance. But that means a lot of polish to keep the vehicle looking clean!

TRUCK SHAPES

In the days before power-assisted controls, truck driving was a job for big, strong people—usually men. The trucks were designed to look masculine, powerful, and even menacing, with boxlike shapes. However, these designs are very bad at pushing aside air smoothly. For every half a mile a big, boxy truck travels, it must push aside about 20 tons of air. This high amount of resistance uses up huge amounts of fuel. Modern trucks have more curved, streamlined shapes to save fuel.

Exhaust stack
Exhaust fumes are dangerous—deadly if breathed in—because they contain poisonous gases such as carbon monoxide. They must be vented from an opening higher than all occupied parts of the vehicle. So this exhaust stack is about 11ft (4m) high!

Sleeper
This eighteen-wheeler has a small room just behind the driver's cab. It has beds cabinets, a sink, and a small stove. On long trips, the driver and co-driver can rest here or pull into an overnight truck stop.

DAYS ON THE ROAD
Truck drivers may spend days driving their rig from coast to coast, so small personal comforts are very important.

Wheels
The enormous wheels and tires are chest-high to an adult. Some trucks have two pairs of front wheels, one behind the other—and both pairs turn with the steering wheel.

Artic link
The truck is designed to haul a trailer equipped with an articulated link, sometimes called the "fifth wheel." The front of the trailer hooks into and rests on a large metal disc at the rear of the truck itself, which is known as the tractor unit. This allows the whole vehicle to bend at the artic link.

Fuel tank
The fuel tank is made of shiny chrome (on a working truck it would be dull gray or black). It holds more than 140gal (2,000l) of diesel fuel, which is 40 times as much as an ordinary car.

Electrics and hydraulics
The rear of the truck has connectors and sockets for the wires and hydraulic hoses on the trailer unit. These allow the driver to control the lights, brakes, and other equipment on the trailer.

POWERED EVERYTHING

A large vehicle like this truck is so big and heavy that the steering, brakes, and other features are powered or power-assisted. For example, the driver puts on the brakes by pressing the brake pedal. But the driver's leg and foot do not produce all the physical force necessary to press the brake pads onto the brake discs. Pushing the brake pedal activates switches called actuators that are connected to the hydraulic system driven by the engine. The hydraulic system's oil-filled cylinders and hoses produce the huge force needed to press the brake pads onto the discs.

LUXURY COACH

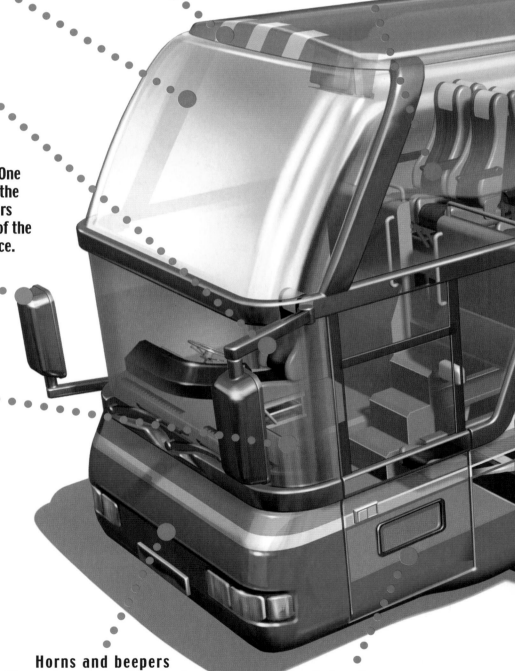

All-around view
The upper half of the coach is panoramic with windows all around, so that passengers can enjoy the views.

TVs and VCRs
A TV screen in the roof at the front shows live programs or pre-recorded videos for entertainment. On a big coach, there is a repeater screen or second monitor halfway along so the passengers at the back can watch, too!

Control console
Like an airplane seat, the luxury coach seat has several controls in the armrest or overhead console. They include a personal reading light, fresh-air blower, socket and volume dial for headphones, and a call button to attract the attendant's attention in case of problems.

Pilot or coach driver?
The driver sits at a dashboard display that looks more like the controls of an airplane. There are dozens of buttons, dials, and lights, with hi-tech gadgets like satellite navigation and a direct two-way radio link to base.

Two-way mirrors
The rearview mirrors may have two parts. One shows the side of the coach in close-up so the driver can see passengers getting on or cars passing. The other gives a much wider view of the background to show vehicles in the distance.

Courier's seat
The guide or courier may sit in a small seat at the front near the driver. He or she is an expert on the area, speaks the local languages, points out places of interest, and gives advice to the passengers.

KILLING TIME
Boredom is a big problem on long road trips, especially through prairie regions where the only scenery is wheat! Some luxury coaches have fold-down tables in an "office area" where passengers can work, read, and use laptop computers (sometimes for games). There are also TVs with VCRs to watch, radio channels to listen to, and books, magazines, or games consoles to borrow from the coach library.

Horns and beepers
The air horn makes its noise by blasting compressed air through a trumpet-shaped tube. It's loud! Also as the coach reverses, the warning beepers sound and the lights flash.

Auto-door
The main door opens and closes by hydraulic levers when the driver presses a button. It slides close to the coach's side so it does not knock passengers over.

All drivers of road PSVs (public service vehicles) such as coaches and taxis have to obey strict guidelines. They can only drive for so many hours, then they must rest for some time. The coach is fitted with a tachometer. An advanced tachometer records the time, the distance the coach has traveled, and its speed at various intervals on the route. If it is linked to the global satellite navigation system it can even record every road! The tachometer is in a sealed box and inspectors can examine it at any time to check that the driver is working safely.

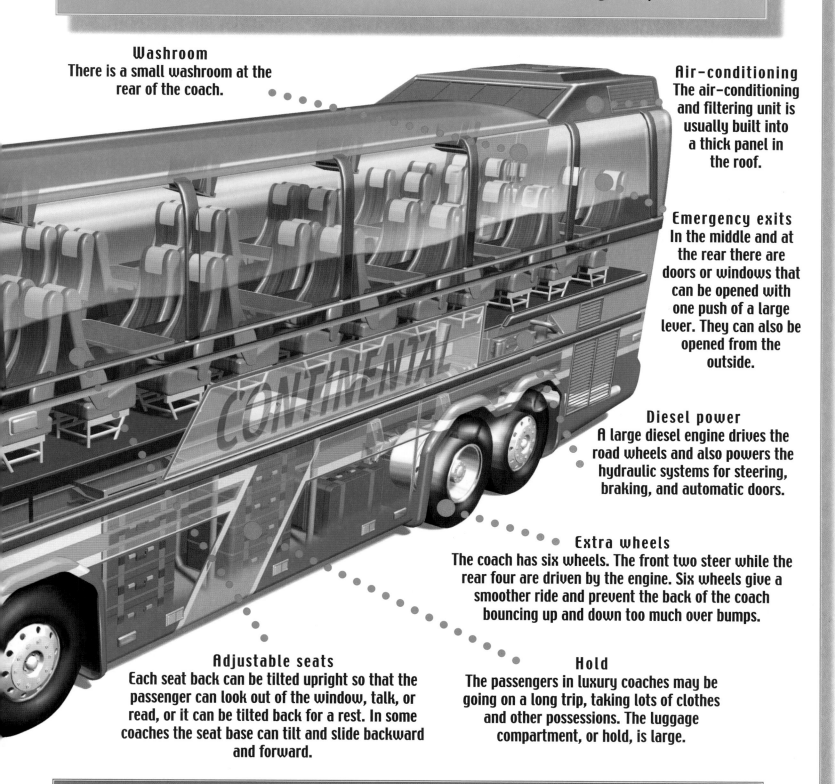

Washroom
There is a small washroom at the rear of the coach.

Air-conditioning
The air-conditioning and filtering unit is usually built into a thick panel in the roof.

Emergency exits
In the middle and at the rear there are doors or windows that can be opened with one push of a large lever. They can also be opened from the outside.

Diesel power
A large diesel engine drives the road wheels and also powers the hydraulic systems for steering, braking, and automatic doors.

Extra wheels
The coach has six wheels. The front two steer while the rear four are driven by the engine. Six wheels give a smoother ride and prevent the back of the coach bouncing up and down too much over bumps.

Adjustable seats
Each seat back can be tilted upright so that the passenger can look out of the window, talk, or read, or it can be tilted back for a rest. In some coaches the seat base can tilt and slide backward and forward.

Hold
The passengers in luxury coaches may be going on a long trip, taking lots of clothes and other possessions. The luggage compartment, or hold, is large.

FLY-DRIVE

Luxury coaches run many regular passenger routes. They are also rented by companies and organizations for outings or special business trips. Dance companies, orchestras, rock bands, and sports teams also use them. But why drive instead of fly? A coach can pick you up and deliver you to the door. It does not have to wait for air-traffic control clearance at take-off and landing. Passengers can get at their luggage easily. A coach is especially useful for hopping from city to nearby city. Even the best luxury coaches are less expensive than a plane or helicopter. And some people are afraid to fly!

STEAM LOCOMOTIVE

Boiler casing
The main casing is a huge tube or cylinder, a very strong shape to withstand the pressure of the boiling water and steam inside. The main boiler section has combustion gas tubes running through it.

Chimney (stack)
This allows smoke and gases from the firebox to escape into the air.

Superheated steam pipe
After the steam has passed through the superheating pipes it is collected by this larger pipe and taken down to the valves and piston below.

Smoke box
Smoke and hot gases from the firebox pass forward and collect here before escaping through the chimney.

Combustion gas tubes
Bundles of tubes carry the extremely hot gases from combustion (burning) in the firebox, forward through the water in the boiler. This heats the water to boiling point.

Valve gear
The valves slide backward and then forward to allow the high-pressure steam into one end of the cylinder and then the other.

Valve rod
This rod is linked to the crosshead below and the radius rod behind it. It is pushed back and forth to move the steam valves just in front of it.

Double acting piston
The piston and its rod slide back and forth inside their tubular case, the cylinder. The piston is alternately pushed from the front and then from the rear as superheated steam is let through by the valve above—this is called "double action."

Crosshead
The crosshead connects the piston rod to the connecting rod and slides back and forth in guide grooves.

Main connecting rod
The "con rod" is pushed back and forth at the front by the piston and its rod, and makes the central large wheel turn around at its rear end.

THE FIRST STEAM TRAINS

The very first railway trains were pulled by steam locomotives. They ran in the 1800s in England, and carried mined coal and rocks. The first passenger steam trains were also hauled by steam locomotives, beginning in 1825 with the Stockton-Darlington railway in Northeast England. During the 1830s, railroads spread across North America and Europe. This was the "Age of Steam." The locomotives were tough, fairly easy to build and maintain, and burned a variety of easily-obtained fuels. But they were wasteful of energy since much of the heat escapes through the chimney, and their smoke and sparks damaged the countryside.

Steam dome and collector
Steam from the boiling water in the boiler collects here and is forced down into the collector and on into the superheating pipes.

Superheating pipes
After steam has been collected in the steam dome, it passes through these pipes, which carry it through the combustion gas tubes. This makes the steam even hotter, or superheated.

Firebox
Solid fuel such as wood or coal burns to create incredibly hot gases that surge forward through the combustion gas tubes in the boiler.

Fire door
The crew open this door to add more fuel to the fire, then quickly close it again.

Radius rod
Joined to the eccentric rod behind it by the expansion link, this is pushed back and forth as the wheel turns. It is also linked to the valve gear in front of it, which switches the steam from one side of the piston to the other.

Eccentric rod
Joined to the radius rod in front of it by the expansion link, this is pushed back and forth as the wheel turns. With the radius rod, it allows the driver to control the train's speed and also put the locomotive into reverse.

Drive link
This long beam with three pivots transmits the turning force of the central large wheel to the large wheels in front and behind it, so all three are driven and rotate at the same speed.

STEAM TRAINS TODAY

In the early 1900s, the Age of Steam began to fade. The first diesel trains were introduced in Germany in 1913. In the same year, diesel-electric trains came to Sweden and electric trains followed in 1915. But steam locomotives still puff along many of the world's railroads. Some are strong and reliable workhorses in remote places where there is little modern engineering equipment to maintain complicated diesel engines and electric motors. Others are tourist attractions.

MOUNTAIN RAILWAY

Pantograph contact
The sliding bar contact picks up electricity from the current wire. The folding arm keeps the bar in good contact with the current wire to keep the electricity flowing and reduce sparks.

Suspension cable and current wire
A strong suspension cable holds up a current wire designed to carry the electric current.

Insulator
Ceramic insulators keep electricity from leaking down the pylon into the ground. They are shaped like stacked cones so that water and ice do not build up on them, causing a short circuit.

Passenger door
Passengers enter and leave by many doors along the side of the car. This makes station stops quicker.

HIGHER AND CHEAPER

Mountain railways are difficult to build and maintain. The track must be fairly straight and may have to be blasted out of the steep rock. It is a constant battle to keep snow and ice off the track and the overhead power wires often ice up, too. A cheaper alternative for some regions, especially tourist resorts and winter sports centers, is the cable car. This is not affected by snow and ice on the ground. It can't work in very windy or stormy weather, but few vacationers are out in this type of weather.

Snow shovels
Angled blades push loose snow off the rails and out of the way as the car moves along.

De-icer
Chemical sprays remove ice from the track and rack so the car can keep moving even in very cold conditions.

Motor
The electric motor runs on current picked up from the overhead wire. Sets or trains of gears connect it to the rack drive cog and the main wheels of the car. The motor can help braking by altering the way electricity flows through it so that they resist being turned instead of causing a turning motion. This is known as rheostatic braking, and adds to the general braking system so the car does not race away downhill.

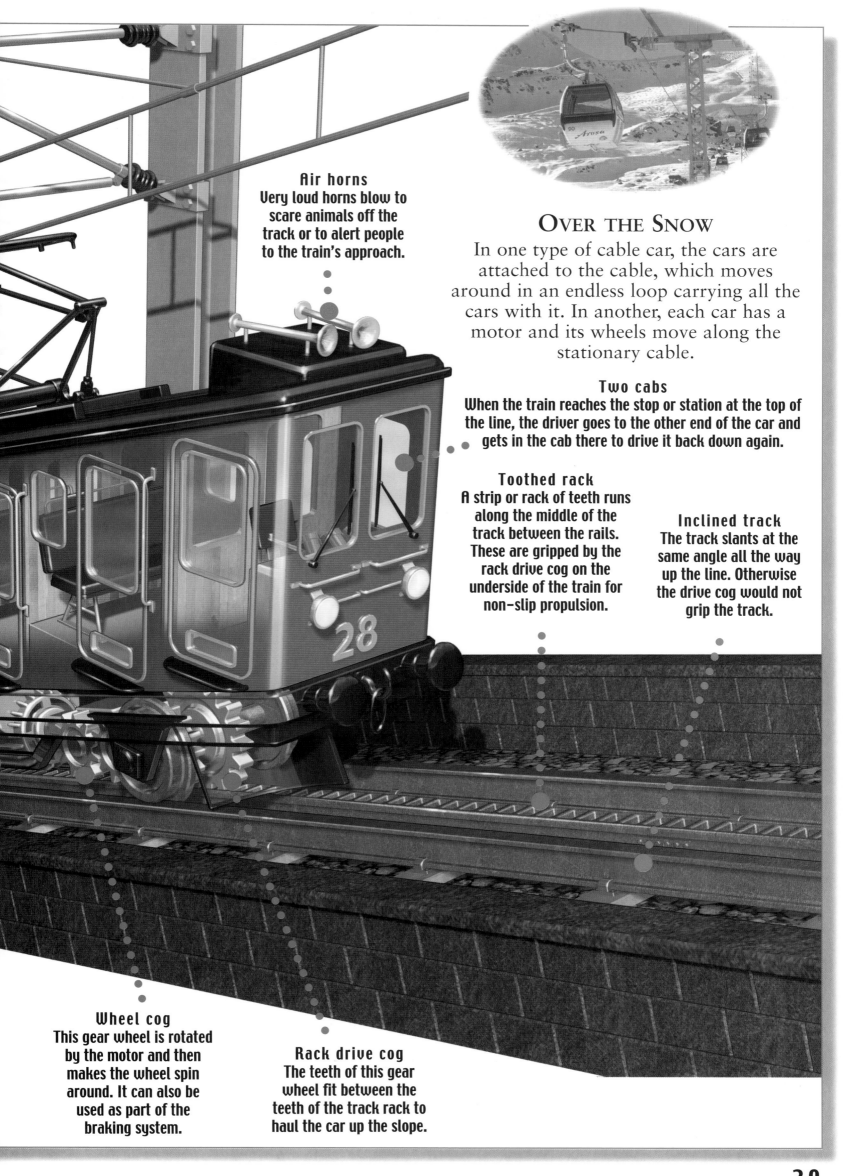

Air horns
Very loud horns blow to
scare animals off the
track or to alert people
to the train's approach.

OVER THE SNOW

In one type of cable car, the cars are
attached to the cable, which moves
around in an endless loop carrying all the
cars with it. In another, each car has a
motor and its wheels move along the
stationary cable.

Two cabs
When the train reaches the stop or station at the top of
the line, the driver goes to the other end of the car and
gets in the cab there to drive it back down again.

Toothed rack
A strip or rack of teeth runs
along the middle of the
track between the rails.
These are gripped by the
rack drive cog on the
underside of the train for
non–slip propulsion.

Inclined track
The track slants at the
same angle all the way
up the line. Otherwise
the drive cog would not
grip the track.

Wheel cog
This gear wheel is rotated
by the motor and then
makes the wheel spin
around. It can also be
used as part of the
braking system.

Rack drive cog
The teeth of this gear
wheel fit between the
teeth of the track rack to
haul the car up the slope.

SUBWAY TRAIN

GOING UNDERGROUND

The first subway, or underground railway system, opened in London, England in 1863. The trains were hauled by steam locomotives so they were noisy, smoky, and sooty. The tunnels were more like shallow trenches with roofs, with ventilation shafts along the route. As electricity took over, the London underground system was converted, and many other cities followed.

Subways carry people quickly and avoid the traffic jams and bad weather at ground level. But the tunnels and the elevators to take people down and up to the stations are expensive to build. The longest subway network is the London Underground with over 250mi (400km) of track, about 120mi (190km) actually under ground level.

Traction motor
Each wheel has its own electric motor that turns it around to move the train forward. The motors of all the wheels are linked by electric control circuits so that they all turn at the same speed.

Hanging rail
Passengers who have to stand can hold onto this rail near the roof, so that they do not fall as the train sways around corners or stops suddenly in an emergency.

Headlight
The driver can see ahead in the dark tunnel using the headlights, to look out for objects on the track, or other problems.

Buffer
These metal discs have hydraulic pistons, or strong springs, behind them. They are the first part of the train to bump into an object on the line, such as another train, and they absorb, or buffer, the shock of the impact. If they are attached at each end of each car they also stop the cars in the train from banging into one another as they move along.

Electrified rail
This rail carries electric current to power the train's traction motors, as well as the lights, brakes, ventilation fans, two-way radio, and other electrical systems.

Sleeper
Sleepers are wooden or concrete beams bedded into the ground under the track. They give firm, level support to the track and spread the train's weight along the rails and into the ground as it passes.

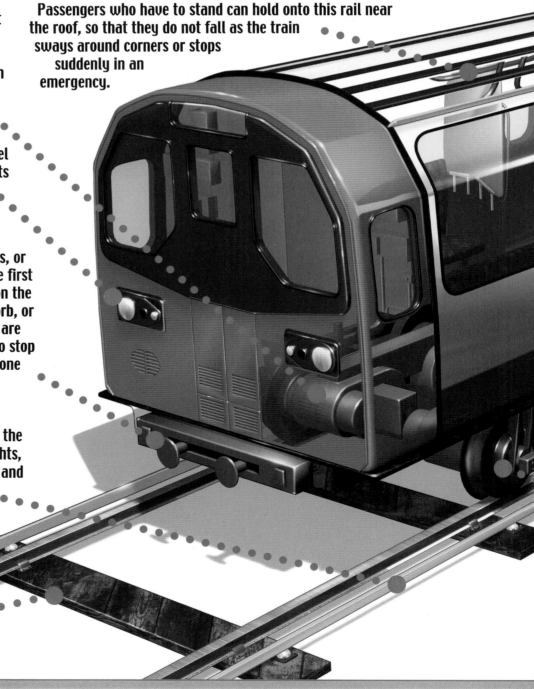

HOW MANY RAILS?

The subway shown here has four rails. The train runs on two. The electricity comes in along a live current rail on one side, and is carried away along the neutral current rail on the other side. Other designs have just one live current rail, called the "third rail." They use the running rails to carry the electricity away again.

Every section of track has sensors that monitor how much electricity is passing along the rails. If there is a sudden surge, possibly because of an accident, the current is switched off in a fraction of a second.

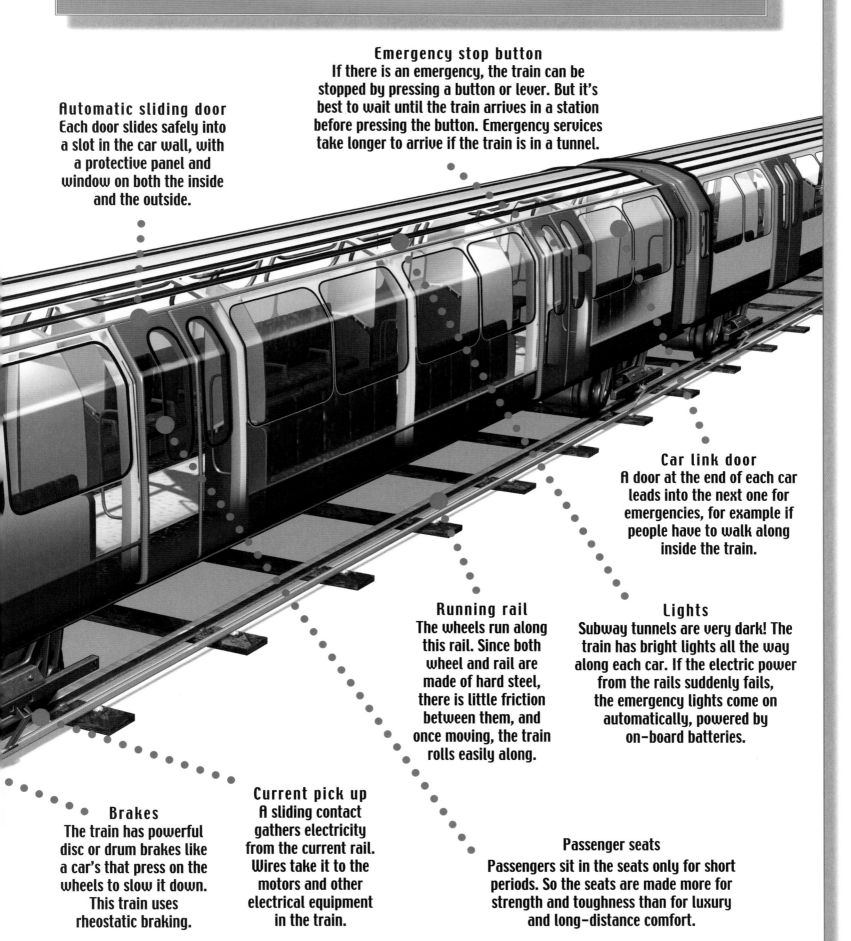

Emergency stop button
If there is an emergency, the train can be stopped by pressing a button or lever. But it's best to wait until the train arrives in a station before pressing the button. Emergency services take longer to arrive if the train is in a tunnel.

Automatic sliding door
Each door slides safely into a slot in the car wall, with a protective panel and window on both the inside and the outside.

Car link door
A door at the end of each car leads into the next one for emergencies, for example if people have to walk along inside the train.

Running rail
The wheels run along this rail. Since both wheel and rail are made of hard steel, there is little friction between them, and once moving, the train rolls easily along.

Lights
Subway tunnels are very dark! The train has bright lights all the way along each car. If the electric power from the rails suddenly fails, the emergency lights come on automatically, powered by on-board batteries.

Brakes
The train has powerful disc or drum brakes like a car's that press on the wheels to slow it down. This train uses rheostatic braking.

Current pick up
A sliding contact gathers electricity from the current rail. Wires take it to the motors and other electrical equipment in the train.

Passenger seats
Passengers sit in the seats only for short periods. So the seats are made more for strength and toughness than for luxury and long-distance comfort.

TGV

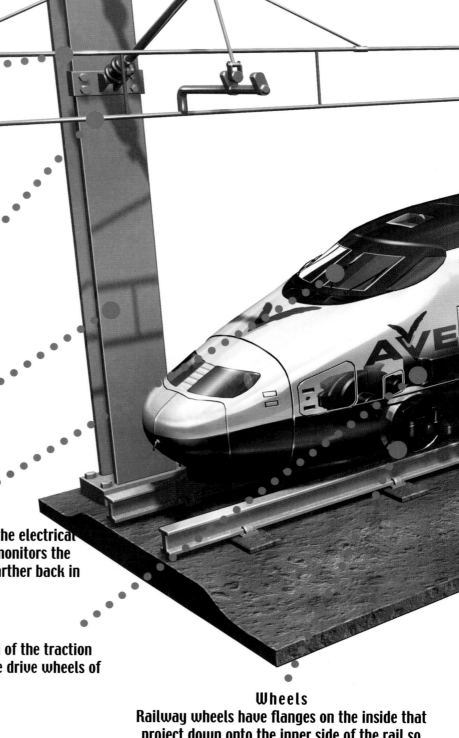

Suspension (catenary) cable
This cable holds and supports the current wire below it. The suspension cable is made of metals designed to withstand the strain of hanging and being blown around by the wind. The current wire is weaker, but made of metals able to carry, or conduct, electricity well.

Current (power) wire
This carries the very high voltages of electric current picked up by the train as it passes below. The current strength may be 25,000 volts or more—2,000 times the strength of normal household mains electricity.

Pylon
Tall towers made of steel or concrete beams hold up the electric power lines.

Driver's cab
The driver's display monitors the conditions in the electrical circuits, motors, and other equipment. It also monitors the brakes, automatic doors, and other machinery farther back in the passenger cars.

Drive gear train
Gear wheels slow down the spinning motion of the traction motors and make it more powerful to turn the drive wheels of the power car.

Wheels
Railway wheels have flanges on the inside that project down onto the inner side of the rail so the wheel does not slip off.

Straight Ahead

High-speed trains must have even straighter tracks than normal trains—with very gradual curves—or they would tip over as they went around corners.

FASTER TRAINS

Modern electric passenger trains whiz through city and countryside at tremendous speed. The French TGV (*train à grande vitesse* or "very fast train") has reached 320mph (515kph) on a special speed run. Other high-speed services that reach 190mph (300kph) include the Eurostar between Britain and Continental Europe through the Channel Tunnel, ICE in Germany, and the Bullet trains in Japan.

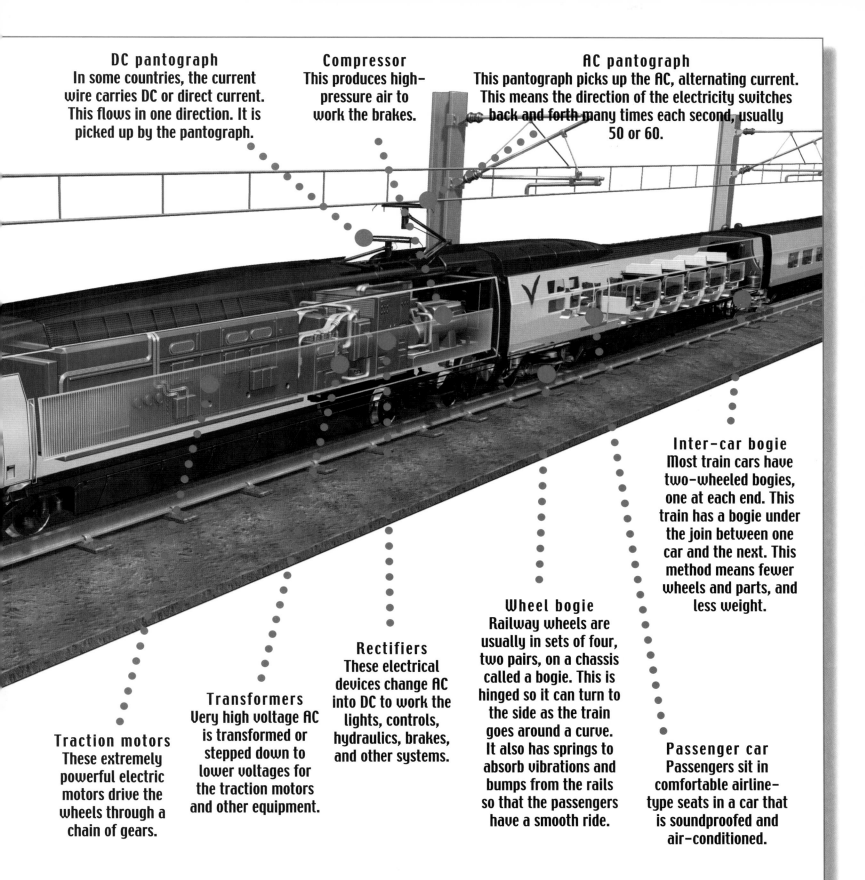

DC pantograph
In some countries, the current wire carries DC or direct current. This flows in one direction. It is picked up by the pantograph.

Compressor
This produces high-pressure air to work the brakes.

AC pantograph
This pantograph picks up the AC, alternating current. This means the direction of the electricity switches back and forth many times each second, usually 50 or 60.

Inter-car bogie
Most train cars have two-wheeled bogies, one at each end. This train has a bogie under the join between one car and the next. This method means fewer wheels and parts, and less weight.

Wheel bogie
Railway wheels are usually in sets of four, two pairs, on a chassis called a bogie. This is hinged so it can turn to the side as the train goes around a curve. It also has springs to absorb vibrations and bumps from the rails so that the passengers have a smooth ride.

Rectifiers
These electrical devices change AC into DC to work the lights, controls, hydraulics, brakes, and other systems.

Transformers
Very high voltage AC is transformed or stepped down to lower voltages for the traction motors and other equipment.

Traction motors
These extremely powerful electric motors drive the wheels through a chain of gears.

Passenger car
Passengers sit in comfortable airline-type seats in a car that is soundproofed and air-conditioned.

LOCOMOTIVES

A train is made up of a locomotive, also known as a power car or traction unit, pulling passenger cars, goods (cargo) wagons, and other units behind it. The locomotive is powered in various ways—

• By steam power.

• A diesel locomotive or unit has a diesel engine that drives the wheels through a gearbox. It can be heard changing gear like a car.

• A diesel-electric locomotive has a diesel engine that drives an alternator or generator to make electricity, which is fed to electric motors that turn the wheels. Electric motors work well at all speeds, so a gearbox is not needed.

• An electric locomotive uses only electric motors, as in the train shown here.

MONORAIL

Articulations
The train has joints, or articulations, where it can bend as it goes around curves. These have flexible seals or gaskets.

WHAT'S A MONORAIL?

The "mono" of monorail means there is only one rail or guide track, instead of the usual two for an ordinary train. This makes the track easier and faster to construct and install.

Monorails carry lots of people quickly over short distances in a busy city. They are quiet, reliable, and non-polluting. They must also be able to speed up and slow down quickly between close-together stations or stops.

Pylons
The pylons hold up the track so that it can pass over the city's roads, pavements, canals, public spaces, and even low buildings.

Wide aisles
Most monorails take passengers on short trips through cities, just like the subway train. More passengers can fit in if they stand instead of sit in the wide central areas.

RMTS

RMTs—rapid mass transits—come in all shapes and sizes:

- Subway trains run below the city.

- Light railways are smaller, lighter versions of a normal railway train, with the usual two tracks.

- The monorail shown here sits on top of its guide track and uses central wheels for propulsion.

- Other monorails are suspended, that is, the train hangs below the track or beamway. The train's wheels and motors are inside the hollow beamway.

- Maglev ("magnetic levitation") trains have no wheels. The train floats above the track, pushed up by sets of powerful magnets in the track and train. However, maglev trains have proved too expensive to be practical.

Automatic sliding doors
The doors slide sideways along the car walls so that passengers are not pushed out of the way as they open and close. A safety device in the cab warns the driver if they are not all closed properly, so the train cannot move off.

Driver's cab
Some monorails do not actually need a driver. There are enough computers, signals, radio links, safety devices, and backup systems for the driver's cab to remain empty. But most passengers like the reassurance of a real person driving the train.

Signal warnings
On some monorails, the signals are not only colored lights, such as green for go and red for stop, but also radio signals. These beam from trackside boxes, are picked up by the train's receiver, and fed into the computer and display.

Controls
The train's controls are monitored by the on-board computer. If the signals are set at stop and the driver tries to continue, the computer flashes and sounds a warning and then takes action itself.

Safety handle
If the driver becomes sick or is injured, he or she lets go of a handle that should be pressed at all times. This automatically stops the train.

Running wheels
The train's weight is taken by running wheels driven by electric motors. The wheels have rubber tires so that they run quietly and smoothly.

Guide wheels
Rubber-rimmed wheels on either side of the track press against its sides to keep the train steady and keep it from rubbing along the central track or swaying from side to side.

Rubber guides
The wheels press on hard rubber guide linings to reduce noise and vibration even more.

Single track
This track is made from pre-stressed reinforced concrete beams or sections—concrete with reinforcing rods of steel inside to give extra strength and slight flexibility.

Power
Electricity for the motors, doors, brakes, and other systems can be gathered by sliding contacts from wires in the track or carried on board as rechargeable batteries.

GOING TO THE SHOW
Smaller-scale monorails and RMTs of different kinds are used in theme parks, airports, seaports, sports complexes, wildlife parks, exhibition centers, and big shopping malls. They are purpose-built to carry people between the main event areas, parking lots, ordinary rail stations, and other sites.

JETSKI

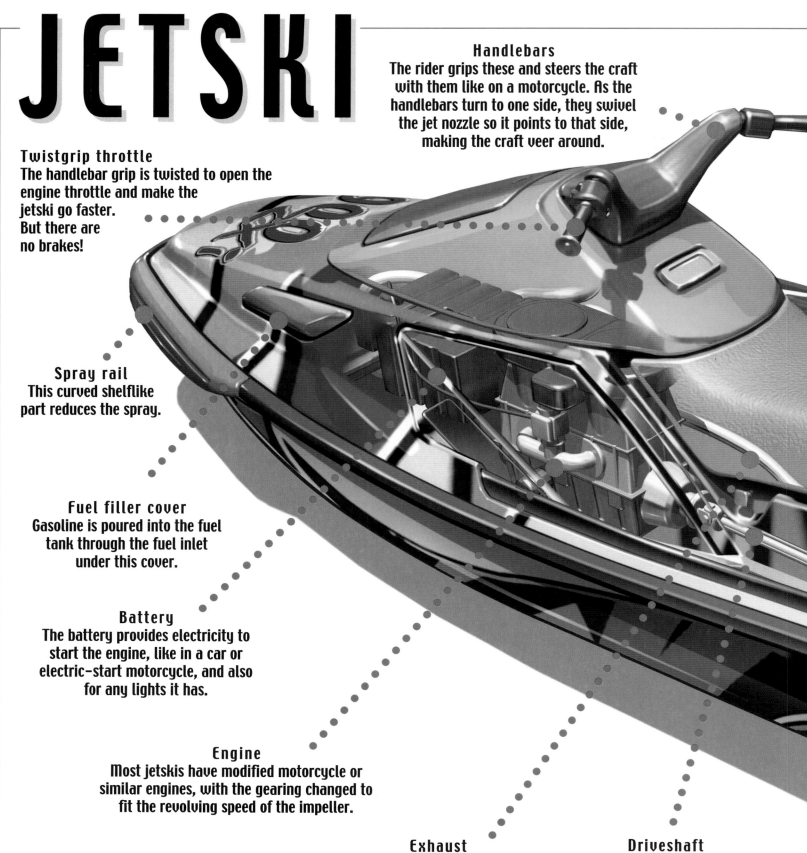

Handlebars
The rider grips these and steers the craft with them like on a motorcycle. As the handlebars turn to one side, they swivel the jet nozzle so it points to that side, making the craft veer around.

Twistgrip throttle
The handlebar grip is twisted to open the engine throttle and make the jetski go faster. But there are no brakes!

Spray rail
This curved shelflike part reduces the spray.

Fuel filler cover
Gasoline is poured into the fuel tank through the fuel inlet under this cover.

Battery
The battery provides electricity to start the engine, like in a car or electric-start motorcycle, and also for any lights it has.

Engine
Most jetskis have modified motorcycle or similar engines, with the gearing changed to fit the revolving speed of the impeller.

Exhaust
The exhaust gases are piped from the engine along the side of the jetski and out at the back—safely away from rider and passenger.

Driveshaft
The turning motion of the engine spins the drive- or prop- (propeller) shaft, which turns the impeller at its rear end.

TRICKS AND STUNTS

The jetski is perfect for all kinds of tricky riding and exciting stunts. Experts can make the craft leap out of the water and spin around in mid-air, or ride up a waterski ramp and do a somersault. Races are held around buoys, often with a line of buoys close together where the rider has to slalom between them. In the group of maneuvers called "submarines," the rider makes the craft tilt nose-up, bounce into the air, and then dive nose-down under the surface, still holding on. He or she can even turn around while underwater and pop up again some distance away.

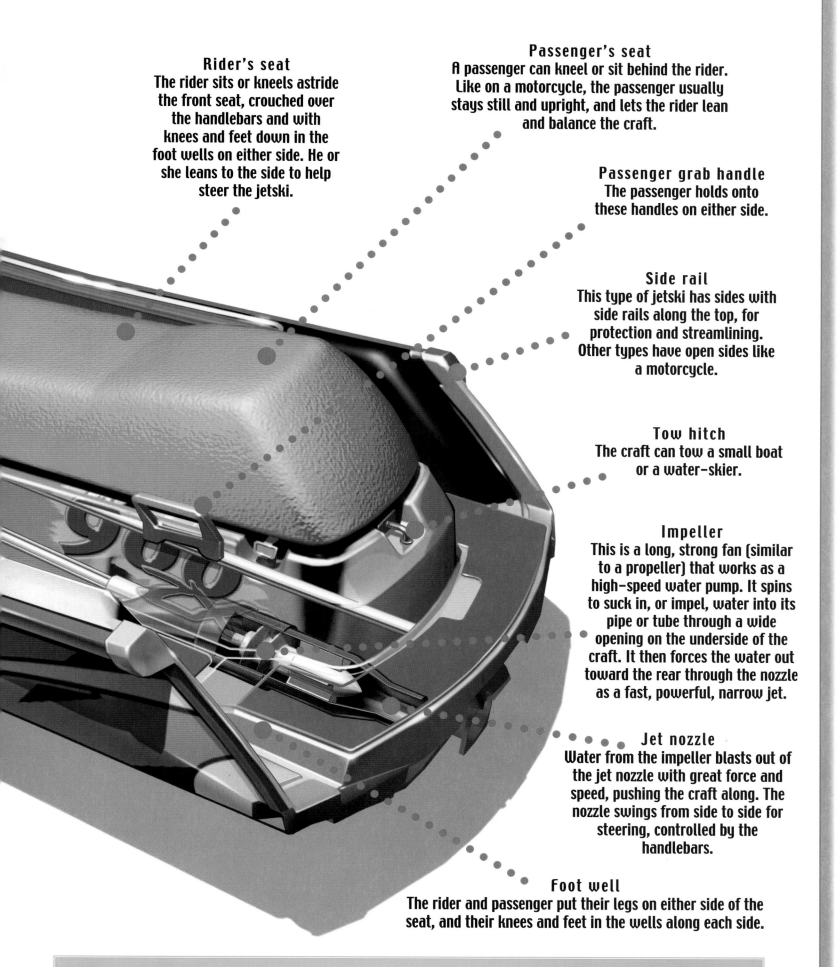

Rider's seat
The rider sits or kneels astride the front seat, crouched over the handlebars and with knees and feet down in the foot wells on either side. He or she leans to the side to help steer the jetski.

Passenger's seat
A passenger can kneel or sit behind the rider. Like on a motorcycle, the passenger usually stays still and upright, and lets the rider lean and balance the craft.

Passenger grab handle
The passenger holds onto these handles on either side.

Side rail
This type of jetski has sides with side rails along the top, for protection and streamlining. Other types have open sides like a motorcycle.

Tow hitch
The craft can tow a small boat or a water-skier.

Impeller
This is a long, strong fan (similar to a propeller) that works as a high-speed water pump. It spins to suck in, or impel, water into its pipe or tube through a wide opening on the underside of the craft. It then forces the water out toward the rear through the nozzle as a fast, powerful, narrow jet.

Jet nozzle
Water from the impeller blasts out of the jet nozzle with great force and speed, pushing the craft along. The nozzle swings from side to side for steering, controlled by the handlebars.

Foot well
The rider and passenger put their legs on either side of the seat, and their knees and feet in the wells along each side.

A NEW TYPE OF WATER CRAFT

Jetskis are like water skis with motorcycle handles and seats, powered by a water jet. They are also known as waterbikes or PWC, personal water craft. They were developed in the late 1960s by American motorcycle racer Clay Jacobson and the Japanese Kawasaki motorcycle company. Their idea was to combine a motorcycle, snowmobile, and water skis into a one-person water vehicle that was fun to ride and race, and didn't cause injuries if the rider fell off. The first craft went on sale in 1973.

OFFSHORE POWERBOAT

Cockpit
The driver and co-driver sit in the cockpit with lots of dials, switches, buttons, and screens in front of them. They rely on these instruments because the waves and spray mean it can be difficult to see.

Strengthened hull
The offshore powerboat is a brutal machine. It smashes through the ocean waves at speeds of over 90mph (50kph). The main body, or hull, must be light yet extremely strong to withstand the battering, since waves at this speed are like sledgehammer blows. It is usually made of aluminum or carbon fiber.

Spray rail
This rail along the hull pushes most of the spray and water aside so it does not break over the boat itself.

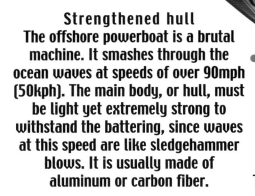

THE RACE

Powerboat races may be around a marked-out course or across the open sea from one town or island to another. This type of racing looks glamorous, but it is very tiring and stressful.

SAFETY FIRST

Speeding powerboats don't lie in the water and push it aside. They plane, or skim, over the surface. Only the very rear parts with the screws and rudders dip into the water. However, the boat can't avoid big waves, and these produce huge shocks as the boat plows through them. For this reason, the crew must tough and in good shape. The driver steers the powerboat, using satellite navigation and many other electronic aids. The co-driver controls the speed of the engines using their throttles and adjusts the boat's trim. The crew are attached to a "kill switch" by long cords. If they are accidentally thrown out of their seats, the kill switch stops the engine so that the powerboat does not race away out of control across the sea.

F1 BOATS

Offshore powerboats have incredible strength and power for racing across the open sea. And just as Formula 1 is the top level for racing cars around a special track, Formula 1 powerboats are the top level on water. They race in sheltered waters around marker buoys, following a course similar to a Formula 1 car circuit, for 50–60 laps. They are small and streamlined with catamarans—two long, slim hulls side by side under the main body. F1 boats have outboard engines, attached by a hinged bracket at the back. They can reach speeds of more than 150mph (250kph.)

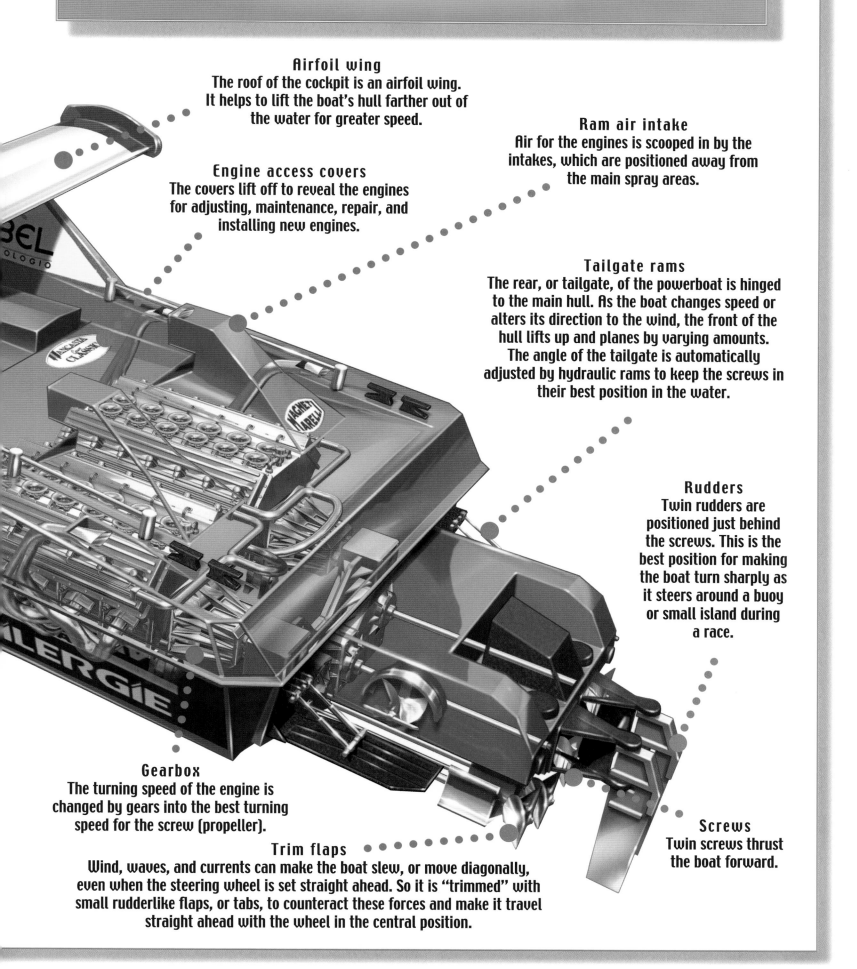

Airfoil wing
The roof of the cockpit is an airfoil wing. It helps to lift the boat's hull farther out of the water for greater speed.

Ram air intake
Air for the engines is scooped in by the intakes, which are positioned away from the main spray areas.

Engine access covers
The covers lift off to reveal the engines for adjusting, maintenance, repair, and installing new engines.

Tailgate rams
The rear, or tailgate, of the powerboat is hinged to the main hull. As the boat changes speed or alters its direction to the wind, the front of the hull lifts up and planes by varying amounts. The angle of the tailgate is automatically adjusted by hydraulic rams to keep the screws in their best position in the water.

Rudders
Twin rudders are positioned just behind the screws. This is the best position for making the boat turn sharply as it steers around a buoy or small island during a race.

Gearbox
The turning speed of the engine is changed by gears into the best turning speed for the screw (propeller).

Screws
Twin screws thrust the boat forward.

Trim flaps
Wind, waves, and currents can make the boat slew, or move diagonally, even when the steering wheel is set straight ahead. So it is "trimmed" with small rudderlike flaps, or tabs, to counteract these forces and make it travel straight ahead with the wheel in the central position.

RACING SAILBOAT

Mast
This is a square tube of aluminum alloy, very light but also extremely strong. It holds up the mainsail and jib.

Jib
The jib catches the wind to help propel the sailboat along and directs it onto the mainsail to make it work more effectively.

Hi-speed winch
Turning the handles of the hi-speed winch pulls on or releases the line to raise or lower the sail.

Jib boom
The boom runs along the bottom or foot of the jib and holds it stretched out.

Jib sheet
This line allows the jib boom to swing to the side by a certain amount so that the jib can best catch the wind.

Side rail
Unlike on most boats, crew members have to move around the sailboat's deck even when traveling at full speed in high wind and crashing waves. The rails keep them safely on the boat. They may also be attached by a safety line.

Bunks
The crew members work a shift or rota system and catch up with sleep in the bunks or beds.

SAILING TECHNIQUE

With the sail set at an angle, the boat can sail diagonally into the wind, which is known as tacking. The sailor follows this direction for a distance then swings the sail around to the other side so the boat tacks the other way into the wind. In this way, the boat zigzags into or against the wind. Sailing across or at right angles to the wind is known as reaching. This is the best way to trap the wind and create the sail airfoil for maximum speed. Sailing in the same direction as the wind, with the sail at right angles to the boat, is called running. Strangely, it is the slowest way to sail—you can never move faster than the wind's own speed.

SUCKED ALONG

Wind blows onto the large area of the sail and pushes it, and the boat, along. But sailing is much more complicated than this. The wind bows or bends the sail into a curved shape when seen from above. The curve works like the airfoil of an airplane's wing to create lower air pressure in front of the sail and higher pressure behind. This means the sail is partly sucked along instead of pushed.

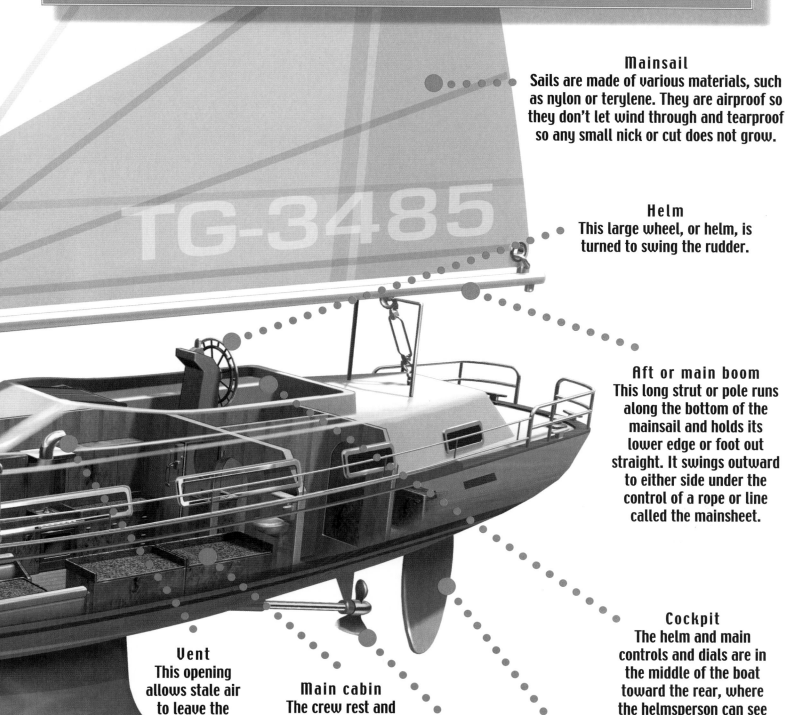

Mainsail
Sails are made of various materials, such as nylon or terylene. They are airproof so they don't let wind through and tearproof so any small nick or cut does not grow.

Helm
This large wheel, or helm, is turned to swing the rudder.

Aft or main boom
This long strut or pole runs along the bottom of the mainsail and holds its lower edge or foot out straight. It swings outward to either side under the control of a rope or line called the mainsheet.

Cockpit
The helm and main controls and dials are in the middle of the boat toward the rear, where the helmsperson can see the position of the sails and how the wind is blowing at them.

Vent
This opening allows stale air to leave the living and sleeping quarters.

Main cabin
The crew rest and eat here. There is also a table with maps and charts laid out for navigation.

Auxiliary power
Most sailboats have a small generator that turns a screw to drive the craft slowly along. This is useful not only when there is a flat calm, but also for maneuvering between other boats and when tying up in a port.

Keel
The large keel sticking down from the bottom of the hull stops the sailboat from capsizing. It also keeps the sailboat moving in a straight line as it leans with the wind.

Rudder
The wheel controls the rudder, making it swing left or right to steer the sailboat.

CRUISE LINER

Restaurant
Many cruise liners serve excellent food and drinks. In addition to the main restaurant, there are also fast-food outlets, snack bars, and cafes. You can get a meal or drink any time of day or night.

Bulkhead
A bulkhead is a wall or partition across a boat or ship from side to side. In case of an accident, the doors and other openings in it can be closed to make the ship watertight.

Patio deck
Deck chairs and tables near the restaurant and bar area are for eating, drinking, visiting, and enjoying the view.

Pool deck
There's no shortage of water—the swimming pool is topped up from the sea. Of course, the water is filtered and treated with germ-killing chemicals first!

Sun deck
As the liner speeds along, the front end, or bow, is very windy, but the rear deck is usually sheltered. Passengers can laze here out of the breeze.

Rudder
This moveable flap steers the ship. If it swings to the left the water pushes against it and makes the rear of the liner move to the right, swinging the whole liner to the left.

Screw
As the screw, or propeller, turns, it forces water backward past its angled blades and so pushes the ship forward.

Engine room
The huge diesel or gas turbine engines are deep in the rear of the liner. Their noise and vibrations are insulated from the rest of the ship. The heat from the exhaust gases is used for the ship's heating system before the gases are sent through the funnel to the open air.

THE "BIG SHOP"

A cruise liner for about 2,000 passengers may have almost 1,000 crew to look after them and the ship. That's 3,000 people to feed and supply with drinks. The ship must take plenty of supplies in case the engines fail and it's late back to port. An average shopping list for a two-week voyage might include—

- 12 tons of potatoes, pasta, and rice
- 25 tons of vegetables
- 40 tons of fresh fruit
- 25 tons of meat and fish
- 30,000 bottles of wine
- 60,000 pints of beer

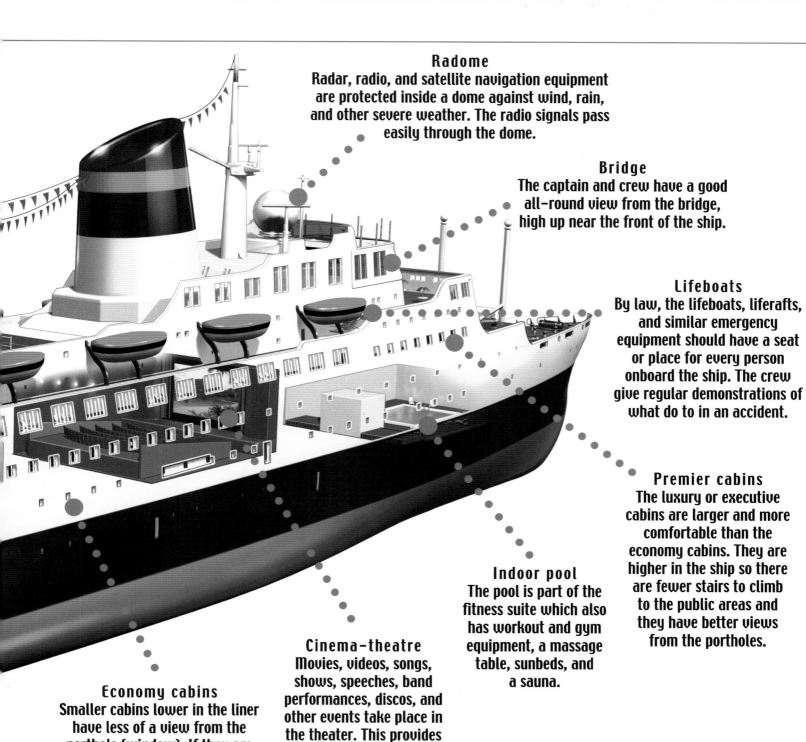

Radome
Radar, radio, and satellite navigation equipment are protected inside a dome against wind, rain, and other severe weather. The radio signals pass easily through the dome.

Bridge
The captain and crew have a good all-round view from the bridge, high up near the front of the ship.

Lifeboats
By law, the lifeboats, liferafts, and similar emergency equipment should have a seat or place for every person onboard the ship. The crew give regular demonstrations of what do to in an accident.

Premier cabins
The luxury or executive cabins are larger and more comfortable than the economy cabins. They are higher in the ship so there are fewer stairs to climb to the public areas and they have better views from the portholes.

Indoor pool
The pool is part of the fitness suite which also has workout and gym equipment, a massage table, sunbeds, and a sauna.

Cinema-theatre
Movies, videos, songs, shows, speeches, band performances, discos, and other events take place in the theater. This provides entertainment in the evenings or when the weather is bad.

Economy cabins
Smaller cabins lower in the liner have less of a view from the porthole (window). If they are interior cabins they have no view at all! This is why they cost less than the premier cabins.

THE FALL AND RISE OF THE CRUISE LINER

During the early 1900s, when few people traveled by air, the cruise liner was very popular. It was a floating hotel that took vacationers to faraway places, which they visited from the liner by boarding smaller boats.

With the rise of jetliners, all-inclusive vacations, and car rental in the late 1900s, people became more adventurous travelers. Cruise ships seemed slow and restricted. You had to go where the captain took you, and for days at a time you were stuck onboard with only a limited amount to see and do.

However, we are now experiencing a revival in luxury cruising, with some of the biggest and best-equipped new ships ever. They are more like floating cities than floating hotels. Now more than 10 million people enjoy pleasure cruises every year.

HYDROFOIL

HYDROFOIL FERRIES

Around the world, hydrofoil ferries take passengers on short, fast trips. The larger ones carry 300 passengers at speeds of more than 40 mph (60 kph). Jet hydrofoils, or jetfoils, have water jets, or turbines, instead of screws. Hydrofoils are especially useful for carrying people between the mainland and nearby islands.

Wheel house
This is where the controls are. They are a combination of those from a ship, an airplane, and a car.

The helm
As in a normal boat, the wheel, or helm, makes the rudder at the rear of the craft swing from side to side for steering at low speed. It also twists the front hydrofoil and its struts from side to side for steering at high speed.

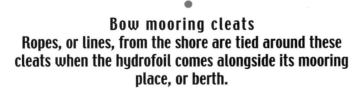

Bow mooring cleats
Ropes, or lines, from the shore are tied around these cleats when the hydrofoil comes alongside its mooring place, or berth.

Hull
The hull sits in the water at low speed, but rises above it into the air on the hydrofoil struts as the craft picks up speed.

BOAT ON SKIS

The hydrofoil is an underwater wing. It works in the same way as an airplane wing or airfoil. Its shape is curved from front to back on top, and flatter from front to back on the underside. As the foil moves forward, water must flow farther over the longer curved upper surface than underneath. So water moves faster above the foil than below. This faster flow creates less pressure above the foil, with the result that the foil is sucked upward by a force called lift. At high speed, the lift is enough to raise the whole craft out of the water. This hugely reduces the water friction, or drag, along the hull, which slows down a normal boat. It also creates a smoother ride. But hydrofoils cannot travel in stormy conditions.

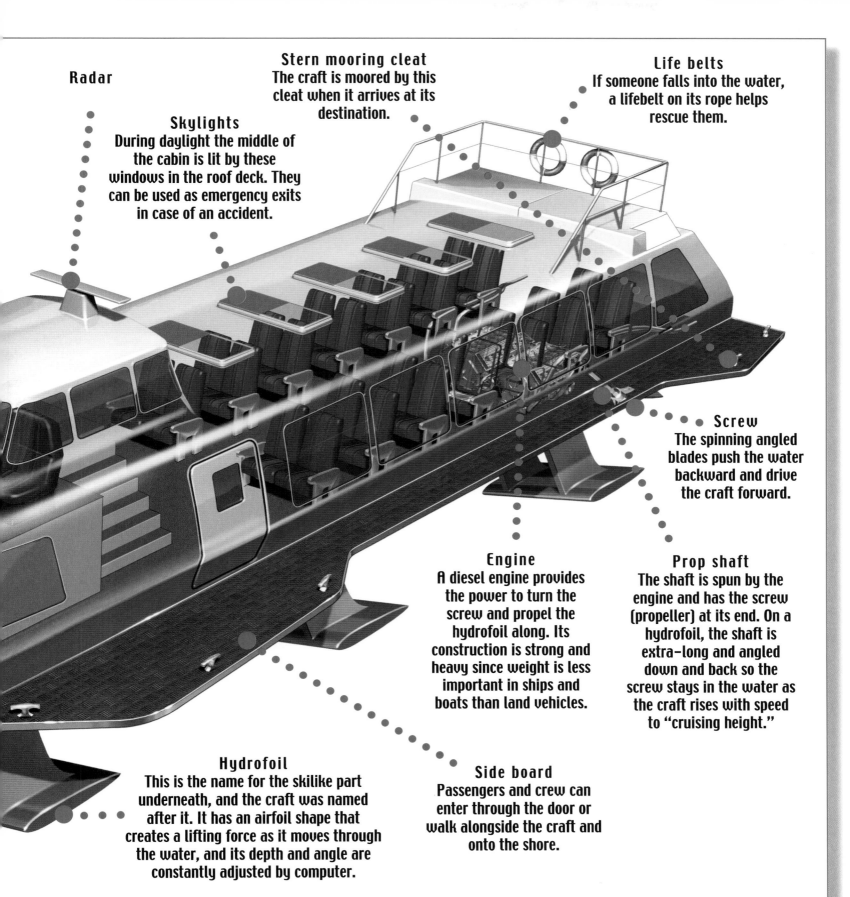

Radar

Skylights
During daylight the middle of the cabin is lit by these windows in the roof deck. They can be used as emergency exits in case of an accident.

Stern mooring cleat
The craft is moored by this cleat when it arrives at its destination.

Life belts
If someone falls into the water, a lifebelt on its rope helps rescue them.

Screw
The spinning angled blades push the water backward and drive the craft forward.

Engine
A diesel engine provides the power to turn the screw and propel the hydrofoil along. Its construction is strong and heavy since weight is less important in ships and boats than land vehicles.

Prop shaft
The shaft is spun by the engine and has the screw (propeller) at its end. On a hydrofoil, the shaft is extra-long and angled down and back so the screw stays in the water as the craft rises with speed to "cruising height."

Hydrofoil
This is the name for the skilike part underneath, and the craft was named after it. It has an airfoil shape that creates a lifting force as it moves through the water, and its depth and angle are constantly adjusted by computer.

Side board
Passengers and crew can enter through the door or walk alongside the craft and onto the shore.

HI-TECH HYDROFOILS

The type of hydrofoil shown here is called a submerged-foil. The whole of each hydrofoil stays under the water. Because the foils are not as wide as the boat, there is a risk of the craft tipping over on its side. "Pingers" along the underside of the craft beam ultrasonic clicks down onto the water surface, which reflects them back to sensors. (This system, called sound-radar, or sonar, is also used to measure the depth of the sea-bed.) The onboard computer constantly measures the height of the hydrofoil and its angle, or tilt, from front to back and side to side. It then adjusts the tilt of the foils so the craft stays steady and safe.

HOVERCRAFT

Drive propeller shroud
The drive prop is contained in a large tube-shaped shroud. This protects it and makes its turning force more efficient by preventing air from spilling out to the sides.

Drive propellers
These propellers push the hovercraft along. The craft is steered by slowing the propeller on one side compared to the other and also by moving the rudders.

Drive propeller engines
Gas turbine engines are used to power the drive propellers and lift fans. They work in a similar way to jet engines, burning fuel into hot gases that rush through a fan-shaped turbine with angled blades, making it spin on its shaft.

Belt drive
A flexible endless rubber belt transfers the turning power from the engine shaft to the drive propeller, or airscrew.

Rudders
The rudders of a hovercraft work in the same way as those on a plane or boat. They push, or deflect, the air to one side and make the craft swing around for steering.

Skirt
The tough, flexible rubberized skirt holds air from the lift fans underneath to push the craft up. The air makes the skirt balloon out and then spills out around the bottom of the skirt.

Stern side door
Passengers board, or embark, and leave, or disembark, through this door.

Lift fan
Large cylinderlike fans suck air from above the craft down through the lift fan air intakes. Then they push it out with great force below the craft, to push it away from the ground or water.

Lift fan air intake
Huge amounts of air flow down through these large intakes toward the lift fans.

Lift fan engine
The lift fans are powered by one or more gas turbine engines under the floor of the passenger cabin.

RIDING ON AIR

Hovercraft and similar craft are known as ACVs, air-cushioned vehicles. Air is pumped to the underneath by large lift fans, where it is partly trapped under a flexible all-around skirt. The increased air pressure below lifts the craft into the air by a small amount. This allows it to move along almost without friction on its cushion of air. The extra power needed to lift the craft is offset by the reduced power needed to move it along. However, the air continually spills out from the lower edge of the skirt so it must be constantly replaced by the lift fans. The first model hovercraft were designed by British inventor Christopher Cockerill in the mid-1950s. The first full-sized hovercraft began its test "flights" in 1959.

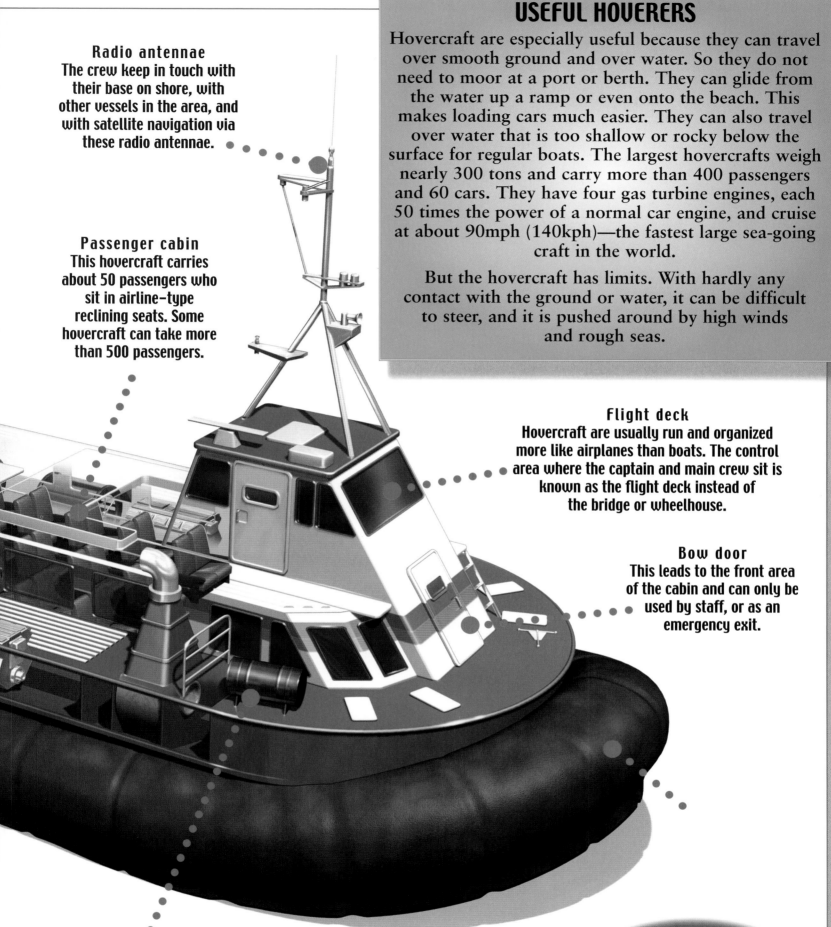

Radio antennae
The crew keep in touch with their base on shore, with other vessels in the area, and with satellite navigation via these radio antennae.

Passenger cabin
This hovercraft carries about 50 passengers who sit in airline-type reclining seats. Some hovercraft can take more than 500 passengers.

USEFUL HOVERERS

Hovercraft are especially useful because they can travel over smooth ground and over water. So they do not need to moor at a port or berth. They can glide from the water up a ramp or even onto the beach. This makes loading cars much easier. They can also travel over water that is too shallow or rocky below the surface for regular boats. The largest hovercrafts weigh nearly 300 tons and carry more than 400 passengers and 60 cars. They have four gas turbine engines, each 50 times the power of a normal car engine, and cruise at about 90mph (140kph)—the fastest large sea-going craft in the world.

But the hovercraft has limits. With hardly any contact with the ground or water, it can be difficult to steer, and it is pushed around by high winds and rough seas.

Flight deck
Hovercraft are usually run and organized more like airplanes than boats. The control area where the captain and main crew sit is known as the flight deck instead of the bridge or wheelhouse.

Bow door
This leads to the front area of the cabin and can only be used by staff, or as an emergency exit.

Life raft
Inflatable life rafts are packed into barrellike containers. They are easily accessible and at the pull of a lever the raft automatically inflates.

BIG DOORS

Some vehicle ferries have large doors, usually at the bow (front) or stern (rear), that fold down to make ramps for loading the cars, vans, and trucks.

SUPERTANKER

The Giant in Port

Supertankers are so huge and awkward to maneuver that they do not come into small harbors. Large terminals are built for them where there is plenty of room and the water is deeper. Small, powerful tug boats push them into position.

Crew gangway
Crew members can quickly reach any part of the deck along the gangways. They often use bicycles, since the whole ship may be more than 800ft (300m) long.

Pipes
A maze of pipes connects the various tanks and pumps with the connectors for loading or unloading the oil.

Pumps
Various pumps force the oil into the tanks when loading at the oil production platform, then suck it out again when the supertanker reaches its destination—the oil refinery or storage depot.

Mooring winches
Thick cables, or hawsers, are used to moor the ship against its platform or terminal. They are pulled in by powerful winches and stored below deck on the voyage.

NEDLLOYD ROUEN

Anchor
The huge anchor is lowered to the seabed when the supertanker needs to stay in the same place but cannot moor, or tie up. The thrusters and main screws might also be used to keep the ship still or "on station."

Thrusters
These small propellers, or screws, in the side of the hull make the boat swing sideways to help with steering.

Valves
The oil is pumped on and off through connectors with valves inside to make it flow the correct way.

SAFETY AND POLLUTION

The supertanker may be gigantic, but it floats easily. Oil is lighter than water and floats on top of it. However, this can cause huge problems. A supertanker accident can release vast quantities of thick crude oil that floats on the sea in slicks. It kills fish, sea birds, and other marine life. If it washes ashore it can devastate coastal regions and destroy coastal wildlife. Newer tankers have hulls with double skins to keep them from leaking oil in an accident, and they also have very strict fire precautions.

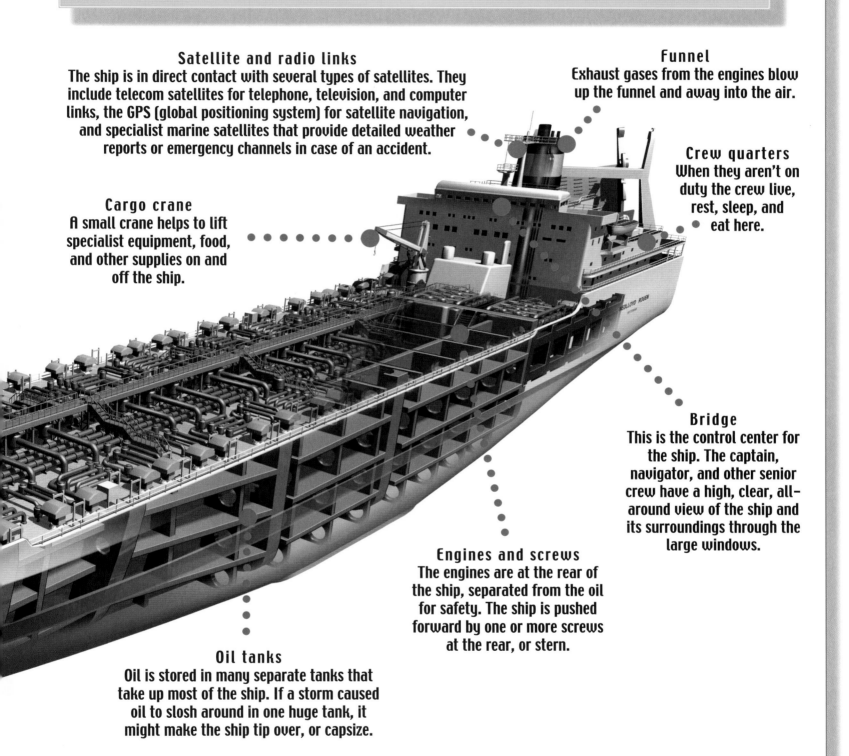

Satellite and radio links
The ship is in direct contact with several types of satellites. They include telecom satellites for telephone, television, and computer links, the GPS (global positioning system) for satellite navigation, and specialist marine satellites that provide detailed weather reports or emergency channels in case of an accident.

Funnel
Exhaust gases from the engines blow up the funnel and away into the air.

Crew quarters
When they aren't on duty the crew live, rest, sleep, and eat here.

Cargo crane
A small crane helps to lift specialist equipment, food, and other supplies on and off the ship.

Bridge
This is the control center for the ship. The captain, navigator, and other senior crew have a high, clear, all-around view of the ship and its surroundings through the large windows.

Engines and screws
The engines are at the rear of the ship, separated from the oil for safety. The ship is pushed forward by one or more screws at the rear, or stern.

Oil tanks
Oil is stored in many separate tanks that take up most of the ship. If a storm caused oil to slosh around in one huge tank, it might make the ship tip over, or capsize.

GIANTS OF THE SEAS

Crude oil is used to make fuels such as gasoline, diesel, kerosene, and paraffin, as well as tars and bitumen for roads, paints and pigments, plastics, mineral rubber, and hundreds of other substances. Many oil reserves are under the seabed. Ocean drilling platforms bore holes down to harvest the crude oil. A supertanker takes it onboard and carries it to an oil terminal where there are storage tanks and refineries for treatment. Supertankers are the biggest ships on the seas. Some weigh over 300,000 tons, and are more than 800ft (300m) long. They take 2–3mi (3–5km) to steer around a corner and 3–6mi (5–10km) to stop. They are sometimes called ULCCs, ultra large crude carriers.

FUTURE VEHICLES

Cars and other road vehicles rule our lives. Their increasing numbers demand more roads, bigger parking lots, larger gas stations, and extra safety laws. They also use up valuable natural resources, pollute the air, and cause thousands of deaths yearly. We all agree that everyone should use them less—except of course, ourselves!

THE END OF THE ROAD?

How long can cars and other wheeled vehicles last? Each year more than 200 million new vehicles take to the world's roads. We are using up the Earth's natural resource of petroleum (crude oil) at a frightening rate. Unless we slow down, in less than 100 years the gasoline and diesel will run out. Electric cars have been developed over many years, but they do not go as far or as fast as gasoline-engined cars.

JUST FOR FUN?

Hopefully there are other options. There is amazing growth in telecommunications using computers, videophones, satellites, and the Internet. This means that we can see, talk to, and send information to people anywhere in the world— instantly. People won't have to travel as often for business. Mass transportation, such as commuter buses, city trains, and ferries will have fewer customers. Working vehicles, such as trucks and combines, will still be around. Personal vehicles will be used mainly for pleasure.

THE HOVERCAR
A huge breakthrough for the future could be the anti-gravity beam. This would counteract the pull of gravity, so the car could rise up and fly. No wheels! It would be like having your own personal helicopter, but much faster, quieter, safer, and more maneuverable. This hovercar would be totally computer-controlled to fly along the correct air lanes, avoid other craft, and find its way by satellite navigation to your exact destination.

MORE AND MORE

One thing is for certain—we will continue to develop new kinds of wheeled vehicles and watercraft. Only 30 years ago, there were no mountain bikes and no jetskis. Inventors are bound to come up with new ways to transport us and our luggage and cargo, to have fun, and to race each other. What might the future have in store? Powered rollerblades? Rocket backpacks? Mini-submarines?

NO NEED FOR WHEELS

One day in the distant future, we may learn how to take an object apart atom by atom and send it along some sort of high-energy matter transfer beam to another place, where it can be put back together again. By transporting a person or object like this even through space, there will be no need for vehicles at all. We could go anywhere, anytime. But what about the excitement and fun of traveling through beautiful scenery and exotic lands? The idea of going on a trip will die away. Maybe we'll miss the old-fashioned joy of being stuck in traffic jams!

PLANEX

Space travel may take people to strange new worlds. Imagine PlanEx (Planet Explorer)—a huge armored vehicle designed to cross almost any terrain as it searches through new regions. It might travel underwater and also withstand explosions, harmful rays, and attack by animals, aliens, or germs. Inside, it could have living and working areas and enough fuel, air, food, water, and other supplies for 10 people for one year. PlanEx may even be in development now! It could soon be ready for testing on Earth in deserts and mountainous regions.

SYMBOL OF WEALTH

Many people dream about owning a fast, powerful sports car, a status symbol for leisure and pleasure. While there are still people who want to show off, there will always be powerful sports cars.

GLOSSARY

4WD four-wheel drive, when all four wheels of a vehicle are turned or driven around by the engine.

ABS Automatic braking system, when a vehicle's brakes slacken off slightly then come on again if the wheel is about to lose grip and skid or slide. This slows down the vehicle more safely than a skid.

airfoil The curved shape of a wing when seen from the side, with a greater curve on the upper surface compared to the lower one.

ATT All terrain tire, a tire which has a surface or tread pattern that is good for most types of ground—smooth roads, rough tracks, and even plowed fields.

auger A corkscrew-shaped device like a drill bit that turns around and bores a large hole, lifting the drilled material (like soil) out and away as it goes.

bogie A small sub-frame or sub-chassis under a main one that carries two, four, or more wheels and can swivel or pivot on its own.

bulkhead A wall or partition across a ship that can be made watertight to stop any water that gets into the ship from flooding along its whole length.

caliper A device with two rigid arms pivoted at one end, usually in a V or C shape, so the open ends can close together.

CAT Also known as a catalytic converter. This piece of equipment absorbs some of the more dangerous exhaust fumes. Most family cars have CATs now.

catenary The curved shape made by a flexible cable, wire, or rope held up only at each end, as in a suspension bridge.

CB radio Citizen's band radio, a two-way radio system that can be used by the public instead of being reserved for special use such as by the emergency services or professional broadcasters.

chassis The main framework or "skeleton" of a vehicle or structure that provides it with strength and support.

cylinder An object shaped like a hollow rod or tube, usually with a piston moving back and forth inside it.

damper A device that reduces vibrations.

fairings Outer body parts that are shaped and smoothed for streamlining, to cover sticking-out parts and sharp corners and edges, and therefore cut down on wind resistance or drag.

FWD Front wheel drive, when only the front wheels of a vehicle are driven or turned by the engine.

GPS Global positioning system for what is called "satellite navigation." A network of satellites going around the Earth enables people on the ground to pinpoint their positions.

hawser A large, strong rope or cable, used for tying up big ships.

horsepower A measure of power produced by an engine, motor, or similar device. A typical small family car engine is about 80 horsepower.

hydraulic A device that works with oil or a similar liquid under pressure, and which usually can exert great pressure or force itself, such as a car's brakes or a car-crusher.

jetfoil A hydrofoil (boat on "skis") powered by a waterjet instead of the usual revolving propeller or water screw.

limiter A device that limits the movement or action of another, usually for control purposes and to keep the machine from "running away" too fast and damaging itself.

maglev Magnetic levitation, when an object is raised or held up without physical contact, by magnetic forces.

monohull A ship or boat with the usual single hull, as opposed to multihulls like the catamaran.

pantograph An extending system of levers, used for many purposes such as copying drawings at different sizes, collecting electrical current from the overhead wires in an electric train, or reaching an object to pick it up with a "lazy hands" device.

pillion A second, or passenger, seat behind the main rider's seat, like on a motorcycle.

pneumatic A device worked by air or a similar gas under pressure, from a road jackhammer or "pneumatic" road drill, to the huge brakes on high-speed trains.

power assistance When a person controls a machine, such as turning on a car's brakes, but an engine or motor is also switched on to give extra power because the human body's physical strength alone may not be enough.

PSV Public service vehicle, a vehicle approved for carrying members of the public, such as a bus or train.

PWC Personal water craft, a small water craft such as a jetski or waterbike designed to carry and be operated by one person.

radome Radar or radio dome, a dome or ball shape covering a radar or radio dish, scanner, or antenna.

rheostatic braking Slowing down an electric motor by feeding electricity through it in a certain way, usually in the opposite way to the electricity used to make it go faster.

RMT Rapid mass transit, a transport system for carrying lots of people (or goods) quickly but usually over short distances.

RWD Rear wheel drive, when only the rear wheels of a vehicle are driven or turned by the engine.

stroke The one-way movement, from one end to the other, of a piston inside a cylinder.

suspension Machinery involving springs, dampers, and similar equipment that reduces vibrations and irons out bumps for a smoother ride.

SWL Safe working load. For example, the weight of soil, bricks, or other loads that can be lifted by a crane or carried in a truck within approved safety limits.

tachometer A gadget that measures the speed of a vehicle or craft, usually by measuring the speed or revolution of the road wheels, or the speed of spinning of the engine shaft.

tailgate A rear fold-down door or similar hinged rear part of a vehicle or craft.

throttle A control device that changes the amount of fuel and air going into a gasoline or diesel engine, and in this way control's the engine's speed.

thruster A machine or engine that makes a thrust or pushing force, to propel a craft along, control its steering, or help it slow down.

Index